IT'S NC   S

A West Yorkshire Cricket Anthology

Editor: David Walker

Shalliley Books

The Pavilion
30 Victoria Springs
Holmfirth   HD9 2NB

01484 683196

Cover Photograph by Richard Turner

Published 2011

ISBN   978-0-9569814-0-0

Printed and Bound by
Riley Dunn & Wilson Ltd
Red Doles Lane
Huddersfield
West Yorkshire

ACKNOWLEDGEMENTS

Alan Hicks, retired NHS manager and current Yorkshire CC member, for proof-reading.

Peter Davies for providing much of the raw material. Without his leadership and support, this project would never have got off the ground.

All the contributors.

CONTENTS

1 - Nineteenth Century

2 - Twentieth Century: 1900-49

Not So Serious

Miscellany

Interlude - I

3 - Twentieth Century: 1950-99

Beginnings

Survival and Growth

Professionals

Miscellany

Interlude - III
The Final that Took Weeks and Weekes - Up Against It

5 - Timeless

Beginnings, Survival and Growth

Down the Generations

Professionals

Top Amateurs

Miscellany

Interlude - IV

The Final that Took Weeks and Weekes - Victory

6 - Not so serious

Section 7 - Postscript

Foreword
Gideon Haigh

We Don't Play for Fun was the title Don Mosey chose for his history of Yorkshire County Cricket Club. David Walker's compilation honours the same county but the opposite side of the coin: vernacular cricket in the dales, meadows and commons of the North, where fun is the whole point.

For me, it has a particularly personal appeal. My father and his family are from Yorkshire so, despite a lifetime in Australia, place names like Thongsbridge, Slaithwaite and Hanging Heaton have a certain magic ring to my ear; likewise stories of people called Frank Sugg and Friend Allsop, not to mention an entire team surnamed Booth.

Open David Walker's book, and you'll soon be feeling a wistful nostalgia for the days when people played nipsy, and raised money with whist drives and miles of pennies. But the contributors have brought us into the modern age with talk of 'IT', once thought of simply as Botham's initials, and 'websites', which would have put cricketers of yore in mind of the consequence of spiders in dusty pavilion corners.

Other stories are lent a contemporary feel by recent events. Todmorden president Walter Parkinson is honoured for his habits of saving money by straightening bent nails and recycling wood, not to mention literally making brass from muck by bottling slime from the club grass pit for sale as fertiliser. Turning crap into cash: hell, Parkinson would have fitted well into administration in this era of Twenty 20.

Australians like to think of themselves as uniquely possessed by sport. Every visit to my relatives in Yorkshire reminds me that this is far from so; indeed, that in density of sport per square mile, the county would be hard to match. And fun? You get the sense from this book that there is quite a bit of it about.

Gideon Haigh has contributed to more than 50 different magazines and newspapers, including *The Times*, *The Financial Times*, *The Guardian*, *The Age* and *Wisden Cricketer*. He has written 22 books, including *The Cricket War: The Inside Story of Kerry Packer's World Series Cricket* (Text Publishing & MUP) and *Many a Slip* (Aurum).

Preface

David Walker

This anthology can be enjoyed on a number of levels.

First, it praises the players, professionals and amateurs.

Second, it pays tribute to the efforts of the men and women who, from behind the scenes, enable players to perform at their best. Persistence in the face of stiff opposition, otherwise known as Yorkshire bloody-mindedness. Some articles touch on external pressures: commerce, church committees and vicars, league and cup administrators, sponsors and benefactors. The major theme remains, however, success through people, mostly unpaid, at the sharp end. This relentless bottom-up pressure helps create personal identity; the interplay between individuals and their social environment. Who am I? How do others see me? How am I the same or different to others?

Third, it is a short journey through history. How informal games of bat and ball grew into organised cricket. Despite professionalism, commerce, gambling, and wealthy patrons. Despite efforts by middle-class vicars to improve bodies as well as minds. Despite landowners, railway companies, house-builders, racists, war and a hundred and one other things, cricket clubs thrived and achieved. The influx of top overseas players, amateur immigrants, ladies in administrative roles, computers and bowling machines also hint at the eras in which cricket has developed.

Fourth, it is a celebration of mostly local and amateur writing. Guys who just love to search around and understand stuff. Some have been through Peter Davies' department and congratulations to them.

Fifth, I would like to think that the articles are not purely about informing, but are also to be enjoyed.

David Walker is a freelance writer
Contact: dawalker@doctors.org.uk

Introduction

Peter Davies

It is a great joy to write this introduction.

When Dave Walker suggested the idea of an anthology of cricket writings - based in and around the work of the Calderdale and Kirklees Cricket Heritage Project - I was annoyed that I hadn't thought of it myself. What a great idea! So many people have contributed to the project and so many enthusiastic writers have tapped away on their PC or laptop. An anthology was waiting to happen!

It was Dave's idea and he has seen it through to fruition, so we are greatly indebted to him. He has brought a professional attitude and many key skills to the task of editing this anthology and it has been a great pleasure to meet up with him over the last year or so and chart the progress of the book.

Dozens of people have contributed material to this book: cricket historians and writers, students, and a whole raft of cricket enthusiasts. The project has been an amazing journey - both literally and metaphorically. We've been to some wonderful places and met some incredible people: cricketers, coaches, groundsmen, tea ladies, scorers, spectators, committee folk and many more.

I remember one chap saying to me: 'It's alright me playing cricket and loving my club, but it needs writers and historians to tell the story of my club and my community. And it's a story that needs telling.' So this anthology is dedicated to him and to everyone else who loves local cricket.

Dr Peter Davies
Former Project Leader, 'The Cricketing Heritage of Calderdale and
Kirklees'
http://www.ckcricketheritage.org.uk
Contact: peterdavies80@hotmail.co.uk

Passion

Lee Hughes (Ms)

Counting the months, not knowing days of the week
Watching years cycle while summer's asleep
Playing the game haunts my life and my dreams
The season of football just yields silent screams

Wisdom is gained from this age-old school
Honing our skills as we whack a fast ball
Starting from scratch, no more than a lad
It challenges all, for good and for bad

Learning of life while playing the game
No other pastime could teach us the same
Making us rich by defending the wicket
My one true passion has got to be cricket

1 - Nineteenth Century

From a watercolour by Elspeth Milnes

19th Century

Beginnings

Cricket in Yorkshire before 1830
Rob Light

Cricket in Yorkshire was at a formative stage before the 1830s. Matches were played between teams associated with the region's major land-owners, similar to those of the south-east. For example, The Duke of Cleveland's XI played the Earl of Northumberland's XI at Stanwick in 1751.

A formal cricket club was established in York in 1784 with rules or *Articles*:

> The enclosed named are hereto subscribed do agree to meet upon Heworth Moor every Tuesday and Friday morning at four o'clock until the fifth day of September next for the purpose of playing Cricket, to play for one penny a game and to fine three pence if not within sight of the wickets each morning before the Minster strikes five o'clock, every person hereafter to be admitted a member to pay one shilling.

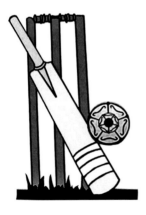

This organisation was clearly aimed at the gentlemen of the city and West Riding teams were likely to have developed along similar lines.

Alongside these aristocratic contests, cricket was becoming popular in the region's urban centres. An account of early cricket by Joseph Lawson, a Pudsey woollen manufacturer and merchant who was born in 1821, looked back over the years before his 1868 publication *Progress in Pudsey:*

… when cricketing was unknown in Pudsey, except as played mostly in the lanes or small openings in the village, with a tub leg for a bat, made smaller at one end for a handle, a wall cape for a bat, or some large stone set on end for a stump (called a hob), and a pot taw or some hard substance covered with listing and sometimes sewed on top with twine or band. They were all one ball overs if double wicket was played; no umpires, and often those who cheated the hardest won.

Like the elite matches of the south-east, early cricket contests in the West Riding were driven by wagers as much as "a hundred guineas aside". Even a contest on Intake Common in 1802, when "a game of Crickets…between eleven workmen employed in the factory of Messrs. Smith, Knowles, Creswick, Tate and Co. at Sheffield and eleven men employed in the factory of Messrs. Goodman, Gainsford, and Fairburn," carried a stake of 11 guineas.

Gambling also occurred in the crowd. When the gentlemen of Howden were comprehensively defeated by the gentlemen of Selby on 23 August 1800, the unfolding margin of victory was reflected in the fluctuating odds which, "at the onset were seven to one in favour of the Howden gentlemen; at the conclusion of the first innings even betting: and towards the latter end of the game seven to one in favour of Selby."

Such *big match* cricket developed a presence in the popular psyche. When Nottingham played Sheffield and Leicester in the 1826 match, the performance of Tom Marsden established him as the county's first star player. Marsden, who was 21 at the time, made a remarkable 227. The innings was subsequently immortalised in a 13-stanza poem by a local poet. The close relationship between Marsden and the crowd, with whom he makes jokes and who later toasts him in an ale house, projects the player into the role of traditional folk hero. A strong contrast with the reputation enjoyed later by amateur stars such as WG Grace. Moreover, the mocking portrayal of the Nottingham fielders celebrates the Sheffield victory; cricket was becoming a strong focal point of local rivalry and identity.

Marsden's status was embellished by his subsequent success as a single-wicket champion, a popular early feature of cricket and the game's purest opportunity to gamble. Matches were made by groups of backers, which mostly pitted professional players against each other for a set purse in a manner which echoed the prize fight. The nature of such challenges is evident in this advertisement which appeared in the *Sheffield Independent* in September 1828:

> Sir-, You will please state in your next paper that my friends are ready to back me to play any man in England a match at single wicket for the sum of £50. The game to be played on the new ground at Darnall, on Monday, the 13th, or Monday the 20th of October; and the person accepting the challenge to receive £10 for his travelling expenses. Upon receiving an answer to this challenge, the stake will be immediately sent to your office.
>
> Yours, & C.,
> THOS MARSDEN.

The publicity gained from advertising such contests shows how these events were viewed as commercial ventures by the organisers, aimed at attracting an audience. Stakes were often advertised at a higher rate than those which were actually paid, specifically for the purpose of attracting a larger gate.

Cricket in Yorkshire before the end of the 1830s was a fashionable pastime among the social elite, also played and watched by those lower down the social order. Whilst the subsequent popularity of a sanitised version of the sport suggests that enjoyment was at least part of the motivation to play, cricket at all levels was also driven by gambling and the spirit of contest. Without these two constant appendages, it is unlikely that 1830s cricket in the West Riding and elsewhere would have developed commercialism, popular following, star professional players and a spirit of local rivalry.

Halifax and District 1826-1898
Andrew Hardcastle

Cricket, like other sports, will have been played in and around Halifax for hundreds of years. The first reference to a match in Halifax was in 1826 on Skircoat Moor, in which Huddersfield were defeated by 30 runs. The first local team to appear in the *Halifax Guardian* was Halifax Clarence, who played against Bradford's Fairweather Green in June 1834, again on Skircoat Moor. Halifax Clarence played their matches in midweek, suggesting that early cricket in Halifax was largely the preserve of the well-to-do who had plenty of spare time. Tradition was that the losers paid for supper at a local hostelry; Halifax Clarence used the *Crown and Anchor Inn* at Bull Green.

There was also involvement for the working man. In September 1834 the Tailors played the Shoemakers on Skircoat Moor (on a Monday), a great crowd of spectators reportedly assembling. The losing Shoemakers paid for supper at the *Labour and Health*.

Local villages formed teams too, playing on Saturdays. First, in 1850, were Queenshead (now Queensbury), playing at Higher Hunger Hill. Others included Ovenden (1850), Mixenden (early 1850s), Sowerby and Copley (1855), Illingworth and Greetland (1858), Elland (1859), Norland (1860) and Luddenden (1862).

Listings like this give the impression that cricket in the area was booming, but this was probably not the case. Many of these sides were probably quite informal, maybe just gathered together for occasional matches. There were no leagues or other organised competitions and most did not become properly established.

One club, Halifax Trinity, did persist. It began inauspiciously with a few games on Skircoat Moor in 1856. The services of a professional were secured and to draw the club more to the attention of the local public, a match was arranged between '22 of Halifax' and the All England XI, a team of touring professionals who had done much to popularise the game in other towns. Several Trinity players were included in the Halifax team, but there were others from Todmorden, Bradford and Sheffield. In a three-day match, Halifax won by 54 runs over 2 innings, a crowd of around 5,000 being reported for the second day, among them many of the leading gentlemen of the town and "a liberal sprinkling of ladies." The venture was repeated the following year, and further matches were arranged against the United All England XI and the Aboriginals, a touring Australian XI referred to in the local press as 'The Blacks'. Halifax Trinity moved to Hanson Lane in 1876 before changing their name to Halifax and settling at Thrum Hall in 1886.

The number of local teams expanded in the 1860s and 1870s, from top clubs with professionals to youngsters in teams with weird and won-

Thrum Hall

derful names like Brook-foot Careless Lads and Hove Edge Merry Boys. Sunday Schools developed teams for juniors, such as Salem Young Men's Club and Primitive Methodists Young Men's Club. Adults were also catered for in new church teams. Works teams were formed: Dean Mill (1864), Brunswick Mills (1862), Halliday & Midgley (boot manufacturers), H Greenwood (carpet weavers), John Crossley & Sons, and Halifax Police (1874).

Village teams for the more serious players grew up at places like Copley, Stainland, Greetland, Blackley, Southowram, but they were not the clubs of today. With no leagues and irregular fixtures, clubs only lasted a short time. Some would re-form a few years later, but others like Mixenden, Mill Bank, Hipperholme, Boothtown, Ripponden Victoria and Moorfield United faded away completely. More durable were Walsden, who played their first match in 1870 and are still going strong in the Central Lancashire League, and Clifton Britannia who were playing in 1867 and lasted to the Second World War.

At a higher level still, competing with the likes of Halifax Trinity, were teams at Todmorden, Elland, Queensbury, Brighouse, Rastrick, Hebden Bridge and Sowerby Bridge. Todmorden played many of their matches in Lancashire, Queensbury in Bradford, and the Brighouse teams in Huddersfield. Local cricket hit the big time for a short spell following the Halifax club's acquisition of new grounds at Thrum Hall in 1886. It was regarded as a high class ground, eight Yorkshire County matches being allocated to it between 1888 and 1898. The climate, rather than the quality of the ground, was given as the reason for it not being used thereafter.

By the mid 1870s cricket results were taking up more and more space in the local press, the *Halifax Guardian* forming a special section for cricket and football. No attempt was made to differentiate between the different levels, the Halifax results appearing amid the rest of the scores. The 1880s brought the publication of the *West Riding Cricketers Guide*, containing the fixtures of around 50 clubs in the area. One was Shibden Hall, who played in Shibden Hall Park. In 1882, this flourishing team considered themselves good enough to undertake a two-day tour based at Harrogate; in 1883 and 1884 they went for a full week and in 1885 for a fortnight.

Burnley Cricket Club 1834-1889
Tony Lister

Known as the Trafalgar Club from 1828, Burnley was founded in 1834. William the Fourth was on the throne of England. The Slavery Abolition Bill and the Poor Law Amendment Act were passed, the latter remedying to some extent the evils of the Poor Law system which Charles Dickens, then a youth of 22, was later to write about. The population of Burnley was just over 12,000, mainly occupied in making common printing calicoes by hand. Communication with the outside world was by road and canal whilst on Healey Heights, gentlemen in hard hats, side whiskers and collars and ties played cricket!

In the early days, many of the club's committee were also regular members of the team and the annual subscription was five shillings! They used several grounds, including Healey Heights, before settling at Turf Moor in 1843. The club closed in 1857 and reformed two years later as the Burnley Wellington Club. The former name of Burnley Cricket Club was revived in 1862/63. Some very good players emerged, including W. Richmond who once hit the ball out of Turf Moor as far as Anne Street, the first street off Todmorden Road. Richmond was the son of a

Burnley grocer. He made one appearance for Lancashire in May 1868 against Nottingham at Trent Bridge. It was not however a success! His *Burnley Express* obituary in 1912 said, "He never entered public life, but socially few men were better known, and none were better company."

In 1863 there was a controversial incident in the game with Accrington. Burnley's professional, Bray, had scored 20 when he missed a no-ball. The longstop returned it, the Accrington wicket keeper made no attempt to stop it and the ball went on to strike Bray's bat. On appeal, he was given out "Obstructing the field". A scene of the wildest excitement followed. The crowd broke on, the wickets were pulled up and the umpire would have been mobbed but for the intervention of the Burnley players!

In 1866, EB Rawlinson became the first Burnley professional to take 100 wickets (115 victims at 6.79 runs apiece). At the same time, 'Little Billy' Rawlinson, to distinguish him from the professional, was the club's best amateur, representing Lancashire in 1870 and 71.

In 1868, George Parr's All England Eleven came to play a three-day game at Turf Moor and duly beat a Burnley side comprising twenty-two players. The local press stated, "For the fair sex a grandstand was erected in the corner on the right of the entrance on Brunshaw Road. The band of the Inniskillen Dragoons from Manchester was also present for the occasion."

In 1874, Burnley (with eighteen men) played hosts to an Australian eleven. The home side managed to score 102 with Spofforth taking 9-55. In reply, the Aussies could only muster 47 for 9. Branch took 4 for 23. An excellent crowd of 3,500 turned up to watch the game. The Aussies were given the gate money of £117.00 and £7.00 expenses and Burnley kept the proceeds from the grandstand, £17.10 shillings.

In 1877, Burnley recorded their lowest ever score when they were skittled for just 11 runs on August 11th at Bacup. A poem was written to mark this unwarranted record and was published in *The Burnley Express*. It reads as follows:

It was August eleven, eleven went out
to conquer at Bacup, but suffered a rout;

Went a Blake, Boys and Branch, and the Tunstills well known,
Roberts, Rawlinson, Richmond, of cricket renown,
with Maudsley and Parker, and Melling, the pro,
In a bus from the Bull in the morning they go;
In high glee they started – eleven the hour –
returned at eleven – sad, sickly and sour,
returned with the fall of night spread o'er the heaven,
and their banner inscribed with the number eleven;
three singles, two doubles, five ducks and a four,
in this way they got up the marvellous score.

Between 1867 and 1883, membership receipts at Turf Moor rose from £400 to £1,100. A bowling green was opened in 1875, a lawn tennis club in 1880 and a permanent grandstand was erected in 1886.

The three famous Branch brothers flourished in the 1870s and 1880s. Fred topped the bowling averages on nine occasions and Tom five, while John Robert was a capable wicket-keeper and later became one of the best batsmen owned by the club. It was Fred who dismissed the redoubtable Australian Murdoch with his first ball when the tourists visited. It's said that Murdoch was disgusted at his own failure and left Burnley by the first train to London, not playing again until his temper had subsided.

Another prominent player was Frank Sugg who scored 164 against Bacup in 1888 and represented Yorkshire, Derbyshire and Lancashire. When he retired from first class cricket he held the record for having scored the most centuries for Lancashire. He was also the centre half for Burnley Football Club, and played for Sheffield Wednesday and Derby County.

In January 1883, the Burnley Cricket Club took over seven acres of land adjoining the cricket field at Turf Moor, allotted it to the football section and presented £65 towards the initial expenses. In 1885, the cricket section complained that the footballers did not clean out the joint dressing room, repair broken railings or contribute any of their profits to make good the losses. The two sections split in 1889 and the football club gained its independence.

Holmbridge 1868-1888

Andrew Pearson

A potted history inserted into a minute book says that there was a club with a ground in Holme in 1868 but visiting teams felt it was "too far out".

A nucleus moved to Holmbridge in the late 1870s to a field opposite the pub (the *Commercial Inn*, now the *Bridge Tavern*) and behind the church (St. David's). This is adjacent to the pitch used by Holmbridge AFC. It is still recognisable as being of cricket field shape although its size is a little reduced from what it would have been when in use. The present field has been the club's home since 1886.

The earliest scorecard in the *Huddersfield Examiner,* dated 7th June 1871, reports on a home game between Holme Bridge Britannia and Little Hayfield. Holme Bridge batting scores were as follows: BA Haigh 16; AP Mellor 23; GH Marsden 2; W Booth 3; R Biltcliffe 12; J Booth 18; L Kaye 8; JA Brook 0; M Bailey 4; C Booth 11; F Dawson 0* Extras 21 (Total 118 all out). Little Hayfield were dismissed for just 12 but no bowling figures were available.

Three of this team, BA Haigh, J Booth and F Dawson, appeared the following season on 25th May 1872 away to Lockwood Mechanics Institute. The hosts batted first and totalled 107 for 8 before Holmbridge, the name now used by the *Huddersfield Examiner*, replied with just 11 all out.

In 1887, a game was played between married and single employees of J Watkinson and Sons (Washpit & Holmfirth Mills) on the Holmbridge ground. There was a wager on the game with the losing team paying for supper at the *Commercial Inn* whose licensee was Mr Willis. The married XI (129) triumphed over the single XI (76), "much to the bachelors' chagrin". According to the report, "The evening was afterwards spent in a manner worthy of the occasion, all being quite in a merry frame of mind". A relatively rare dismissal occurred when one of the married team was given out handled the ball.

Reports in the *Holmfirth Express* of the club's Presentation Dinner in 1954, referred to an incredible game in 1888 when Holmbridge were dismissed for 35 but then bowled out Scholes for just 13. This prompted a letter from someone signing himself as *The Lad from Scholes*. The writer "well remembered seeing that match as I was then a lad from Scholes," The general feeling was that Holmbridge had already lost with such a low score. Fred Lockwood, uncle of Kenyon Lockwood, the Scholes captain, "took some of the Scholes spectators to the *Commercial Inn* in anticipation of Scholes winning easily. By the time some of these spectators got back to the field the match was over."

Five years before writing the letter, *The Lad from Scholes* had met the Holmbridge wicket-keeper on that famous day. The keeper told him he'd stood up to Tom Redgwick who was the fastest bowler they had experienced. His hands tingled as he took the ball. Early in the innings, he slightly overbalanced on taking the ball and touched the wicket with the toe of his boot. On appeal, the batsman was given out and so he tried it again and again at both ends "until he had taken more wickets than any of the bowlers, although the bowlers were credited with them." Things apparently happened so quickly that no one was able to work out what was going on.

On 9th July 1887 there was a game between past and present players. In a low scoring contest, the Past Players' 63 all out of the was enough to beat the 44 all out of the Present XI. Supper was provided by Mr Willis, the licensee of the *Commercial Inn* and a member of the victorious team could not resist pointing out that "nowt beats t' young uns nobbut th'oud uns."

Holmbridge
Daniel Stewart

Holmbridge Cricket Club nestles next to woods which dwarf the pavilion and pitch. On the other side are homes built into the hill on terraces, a dominant man made cliff. It feels like it is in a gully or valley: intimate, enclosed and protected from the outside world.

A Cricket Prayer
Lee Hughes (Ms)

Goddess of sport grant us grace in your sight
To stand firm by stumps and hold bats upright
To block every ball and reach each boundary line
Please lead us victorious and keet weather fine

Good men of integrity raise a glass with your host
For each man of virtue to join in this toast
In honour of bat and of ball and of wicket
Pray we're triumphant in this vocation to cricket

The Heavy Woollen Cup 1884-1885
Mike Butler

Although cricket had been played locally from the mid-nineteenth century onwards, there was little organisation. The first league in the country was established in Birmingham in 1888. The Bradford Cricket League was founded as late as 1903.

The Heavy Woollen Cup was, therefore, a significant step in bringing more structure to the game locally. It also gave smaller clubs the opportunity to play their larger, more sophisticated rivals. *The Cleckheaton Advertiser* reported:

> I am very glad of one thing, that is the way the younger organisations and what were considered inferior clubs are making their mark. If the institution of the Challenge Cup was to serve any good purpose at all it was to encourage cricket and bring forward, to public notice, rising clubs, and this it is doing. This may be specially noticed in the case of Thornhill who, although it has been thrown out by Hunsworth Mills [subsequently Cleckheaton] has considerably improved its standing, and what was hitherto an unknown club, in this district at least, should have no difficulty in arranging good matches for next season.

The 1884 cup ties were played on consecutive Saturdays beginning on the last Saturday in July. The second round provided two major upsets. First, Spen Victoria were all out 84, losing by 52 runs to a Roberttown team featuring an underarm bowler, Hall, who took five wickets. Second was the defeat of the holders, Heckmondwike, at the hands of lowly Dewsbury Moor, by four wickets. A contributory factor was the Dewsbury Moor ground, reported by *The Cleckheaton Advertiser* as being "a very poor one, being small and very uneven."

The *surprise* teams were, however, eliminated in later rounds, leaving Dewsbury & Savile to contest the final against Ossett. Between 4,000 and 5,000 spectators attended the match, played at the Savile Ground. After a late start because of rain, Ossett, according to *The Cleckheaton Advertiser* "piled up the extraordinary score of 211 in 3 hours" and by the close Dewsbury were 12 without loss. The game was re-started the following

Saturday, abandoned through rain, and played to the finish the following Wednesday when Dewsbury were finally dismissed for 165.

Following the triumphs of Heckmondwike and Ossett in the previous two years, it was the turn of Birstall to win the trophy in 1885. Three

match results from the first round are worthy of comment. In the first, Dewsbury & Savile amassed a huge total of 448, no declarations being allowed. In reply, their hapless opponents, Mirfield St. Johns, mustered 15 runs, with one man, Hepworth, scoring 10 of them, to lose by a mere 433 runs! In the second, Dewsbury Moor must have feared their chances of matching the exploits of the previous year were doomed when they were dismissed for a paltry 32. Not so, their opponents fell for 28 with the match being completed in less than an hour! Finally, the tie of the round pitched the previous two winners against each other. The result was somewhat different to expectations, with Heckmondwike all out 32, a total easily passed by Ossett without loss. The major reason for Ossett's

The original cup

triumph was their successful objection to the inclusion of Berry and Usher, two of the best Heckmondwike players, alleging that they were engaged as professionals at Hodgson & Simpson.

Before the date of the second round, it was reported that the Cup committee had declined to allow the publication of the names of the neutral umpires because of fear of bribery or other undue influence being brought to bear. Is this the first report of suspicions of potential match-fixing in cricket?

The second round saw a repeat of the 1884 Spen Victoria v Roberttown match. There was to be no repeat of Roberttown's fairy tale victory, however, as Spen won by seven wickets, having dismissed their opponents for 96. Special trains were chartered from Cleckheaton for Spen's next encounter at Dewsbury & Savile, but a rude awakening was in store. In reply to the home side's 156, Spen could only muster 34, being swept aside by Bottomley (7 for 14).

Batley and Chickenley tied on 110. Chickenley sought to have the replay held either at their ground or the Savile Ground, but the committee decided it must be on the same ground with the same umpires and that Chickenley should bat first. Despite retaining home advantage, Batley were overwhelmed in the replay as Chickenley, maybe piqued by the decisions of the committee, scored 311, way beyond Batley's reach.

Dewsbury & Savile again reached the final and some members of the committee were in favour of a neutral ground, but the proposal to play at Mount Pleasant, Batley, was defeated by one vote. Admission was set at 3d and special trains were run from Birstall. Around 8,000 spectators were present on the first day which ended finely balanced with Birstall on 168 for 6 in reply to Dewsbury's score of 242. The game was resumed the following Thursday in slight rain and Birstall progressed to 220 without further loss, at which point Dewsbury appeared to lose heart and Hill even bowled some underarms. Birstall did lose two further wickets but finally reached 243 for 8 to achieve a memorable victory. Thousands gathered at the *Smithies* that Thursday evening and the Birstall band played *See the Conquering Heroes*.

(The Heavy Woollen District Challenge Cup Committee held its first meeting at the Royal Hotel in Batley on October 18 1882 and made a draw from twenty five local teams. The Cup was open to all clubs situated within six miles of Batley Town Hall)

Beginnings and Churches

Illingworth St Mary's 1884
Dennis O'Keefe

On 6 July 1878, the Reverend William Davies scored 35 not out for St. Mary's Illingworth against Nursery Lane. He became curate of St. Mary's in April 1877, having graduated from Oxford the previous year. Highly popular with the parishioners, it's possible he negotiated to buy or lease the ground at Pharaoh Lane, only a short walk from the church.

In 1878 eight fixtures were reported, sixteen in 1879 and ten in 1880.

In 1881 however, no matches were reported, and in 1882 only two. A revival took place in 1883, commencing with a fixture against Bradshaw St John on 16 June and the *Halifax Guardian* subsequently reported 15 fixtures. On the back of this resurgence, the club was formally established in 1884.

As Vicar of St. Mary's from 1879, the first president of the new cricket club was the Revd George Oldacres. A Cambridge undergraduate in the 1860s, he was acquainted with the *civilising* effects of muscular christianity. He probably arranged two fixtures against the Church Institute of his old parish in Brighouse, but he was not a likely initiator of the club. He made only occasional appearances at the higher profile meetings, a sympathetic figurehead, rather than an enthusiastic supporter.

The curate, Frederic Hughes, who arrived in 1881, was more involved in the running of the club, his professional approach being evident in the early club minutes, setting a precedent of high standards. However, considering the number of fixtures arranged and played since 1877, the parishioners' appetite for cricket already existed.

Drawing by Sue Brant

The general meeting of the club on 22 February 1884 is regarded as inaugural. It is evident, however, that much had already been decided, including the committee and officers, a set of comprehensive club rules, financing "the erection of a Cricket Tent" (wooden pavilion) and the season's fixtures. The February 1884 meeting was more confirmation than baptism.

Rule 3 restricts membership to Sunday School or churchgoers. Rule 13 qualifies this restriction and permits friends from outside the parish to play, suggesting a fear of player shortages at a time when many cricket teams were ephemeral.

Of the seventeen rules, six (no's 6, 8, 9, 11, 12 & 15) have a behavioural-disciplinary element. Rule 8: "That no member be allowed to smoke or lie down when he is engaged on the field" is an example of a *rational recreation* response to pre-industrial behaviour. Rule 9 has a particularly clerical ring to it, referring to fining "any member conducting himself improperly, either by word or deed." Fines for first offences were 6d, the same as the monthly subscription.

Illingworth's rules were a product of Victorian morality and muscular christianity and not something peculiarly strict for Illingworth members. The local church's ownership, though, was explicit. Rule 14 stated that the key to the cricket tent key be retained at the Church Institute and on dissolution of the club, the tent and equipment became Sunday School property (Rule 16).

Illingworth's low subscriptions attracted the working class to the church. The subscription of 5/- pa could be paid monthly on "easy terms" of 6d during the season and 4d out of season. The entrance fee of 1/- would be waived for annual subscriptions. By April, a junior rate had been set. Illingworth was thus an *inclusive* club.

Compare this with Todmorden, founded almost fifty years later. The 1838 membership showed a predominance of employers and self-employed men. They had leisure time and could afford the joining fee of 2/6d and the monthly subscriptions of 1/-, which, though soon reduced to 9d, made the annual cost for a new member still greater than the weekly wage of some workers.

Sowerby Bridge Church Institute 1894-1908
Brian Heywood

Sowerby Bridge Church Institute Cricket Club was founded as Christ Church Cricket Club around 1880.

Church and Sunday School were at the centre of community life in Victorian England and it was common for them to embrace many aspects of their members' lives. When a cricket club was instigated by the Young Men's Class of Christ Church, which met at the Town Hall in Sowerby Bridge, it was consistent with the pattern across the industrial North and Midlands. Most players attended Christ Church and, catering for numerous leisure activities, the Institute was the church's social and sporting arm.

After a decade playing challenge matches against other local teams, Christ Church CC was swept along in the rush towards the formation of leagues in cricket, association football and rugby football around 1890. The *Sowerby Bridge Division Cricket League* was one of hundreds formed at this time and Christ Church was playing in it by 1894.

Drawing by Sue Brant

Possibly to avoid confusion with other clubs of ecclesiastical origin, the club became known as Sowerby Bridge Christ Church and by 1908 was playing under the name of Sowerby Bridge Church Institute, a mouthful quickly abbreviated to S.B.C.I.

Outlane Methodist 1897
Dennis O'Keefe

A team called Outlane was playing fixtures from as early as 1884. The second August edition of the *Halifax Courier* that year advertised a game between Clifton Britannia and Outlane, with their respective second XI's playing at Outlane. The first XI fixture was also reported in the *Leeds Mercury* which was becoming something of a regional newspaper. The *Huddersfield Examiner Supplement* of 30 August 1884 reported a game against Thurstonland, which, unusual for two distant hilltop villages, appears to have been a fairly regular fixture. They played each other in 1887 and 1888 (twice) at the very least.

The *Leeds Mercury* of Monday 11 July 1887 gave notice of the Huddersfield District Challenge Cup first round match at home to Paddock. Other fixtures for the club were also reported, including for season 1892, but none for 1893 to 1896.

It is known that Outlane was fielding two sides in 1884, so the suspicion is that they played more regularly than appearances in the press would suggest. They didn't bother sending details to the newspapers. Perhaps in an outlying and self-contained village it was neither necessary nor worth the effort to notify players of selection via the newspapers. Maybe there were informal arrangements that kept opponents or the wider public informed.

Though playing simply as Outlane, three match reports, Thurstonland (1884 and 1887) and Helme (1887) reveal links with the local chapel and the future cricket club. B. Hoyle is mentioned, almost certainly Ben Hoyle, who was to become both a chapel Trustee and a vice president of the established club.

In 1893, the Outlane Methodist New Connexion opened a new chapel, named Bethel, and a new school. In 1897, the centenary year of the Methodist New Connexion, Outlane MNC Cricket Club was formed. It is unlikely that the church played much part in the venture. More probable was the club's desire to be formal, backed by the chapel's congregation and resources, with the capacity to embark on league cricket. Due to the huge popularity of the new leagues in the area, it was increasingly difficult to find opponents for *ordinary*, that is, friendly, fixtures.

19th Century

The first written record of the club is found in the *Secretary's Book* (a cashbook) on 1 April 1897 and is an entry for the receipt of subscriptions to the value of £3/16/-. The club's rules had to be ratified by the chapel's Trustees (their acceptance being proposed by Ben Hoyle) which was done on 8 April. This is the only direct reference to be found to the cricket club in either the Trustees' minute books or those of the church leaders.

Early Professionals

Tom Emmett: The Illingworth Beacon
Andrew Smith

Tom Emmett is Illingworth Cricket Club's most famous player, one of only four Halifax and District players to play Test cricket for England. The others are Bill Bowes, Gerald Smithson who played for Illingworth as a junior and Richard Blakey. But none, including Bill Bowes who bowled the great Don Bradman with his first ball in Test cricket, made the impact on the game that Tom Emmett did.

Much of what we know about Tom Emmett comes from *Talks with Old Yorkshire Cricketers* by AW Pullin (*Old Ebor*). Published in the Yorkshire Evening Post in 1898, the book contains a chapter on the popular Yorkshire all-rounder, describing him as the greatest character of them all, including Dr WG Grace and KS Ranjitsinhji.

In his interview with *Old Ebor*, Tom stated:

> I lived close to my uncle Dilworth of Illingworth near Ovenden who was fond of cricket. One of the great traders of the place was Mr Henry Ambler, who had a nice carriage drive leading up to his residence. At the entrance to the drive were two stone posts, and it was one of these that we used for our wickets. That was where I was initiated into cricket and where I first found I could hit the post with a round arm delivery.

According to *Old Ebor*, Emmett's first club was called the Illingworth.

The club's promoters were Thomas Taylor, a local manufacturer, and Mark Chapman, the host of *The White Lion,* which was the club's head-quarters.

A further quote from Tom referred to the summer of 1858 when he was sixteen:

> I had removed then to the top of Moor Lane, and they made me a member and took me up one day to field for them. Then they said I should have to bowl, and I began with underhand bowling. Mark Chapman said I should have to give it up and bowl round arm, and I did, and bowled so well that I became a regular bowler for them. I used to bowl very straight then, far straighter than I used to do afterwards. I played in one of the Illingworth Feast matches against a team from Thornton and though I did very well in that match I remember that they used to play my straight deliveries very easily. This set me thinking whether I could give a bias to the ball one way or another and by persevering found I could make it break back a bit.

In 1863, after meeting the Keighley team, he played as their professional. Three years later he left for the local *Twenty –Twos* against the All-England Elevens, making his Yorkshire debut in August of the same year.

Whilst he could be erratic, he was probably one of the first bowlers to use the full width and depth of the crease to vary the point of delivery. He was respected by the best for his ability to produce the unplayable delivery, including what Tom called his *sostenutor*, described by WG Grace "as an impossible ball … pitching between the legs and the wicket with sufficient break and rise to hit the off bail."

No doubt helped by the poorer pitches of the day his first class record of 1572 wickets at an average of 13.57 is the second best of all time for bowlers with over 1500 wickets. According to Derek Hodgson in his Official History of Yorkshire County Cricket Club he was "the best loved cricketer of his day and, after WG, the most famous." After one big innings from WG Grace, Emmett told him, "They ought to mak' thee bat with a littler bat."

Surprising for a working class player, he captained Yorkshire between 1878 and 1882. A terrific County Club minute from 1878 records "that T. Emmett be made captain in the absence of a gentleman." Amazingly he was Yorkshire's last professional captain until Vic Wilson in 1960.

Emmett played for England in 7 of the first 8 Test matches, all in Australia, including the very first Test match at Melbourne in 1877. He toured Australia three times, taking 137 wickets on the 1878-79 tour alone.

He was a regular member of the Yorkshire team until 1887, missing only 14 games in 21 years, helping them to unofficial championships in 1867, 1869 jointly with Nottinghamshire and again in 1870. In addition to his wickets, he scored 6,315 runs.

He was one of the first cricketers to have a benefit match which raised the considerable sum of £620 in 1887. In 1888, he became cricket coach and groundsman at Rugby School. Later, he coached at Leicestershire. Whilst at Rugby, one of his pupils was Pelham Warner. *Plum* Warner,

England captain, knight and President of the MCC, recalled Tom as "a character … with … merry eyes (and) an attractive laugh." He felt that Emmett allowed the boys to develop naturally and without rigidity.

Tom died at Leicester in 1904 at the age of 62. The last word goes to Lord Hawke, Yorkshire captain after Emmett, who said of Tom "… the greatest character that ever stepped on a cricket field, a merry wag who could never lose heart nor temper."

Louis Hall: The Batley Stonewaller
Martin Howe

The longest standing Yorkshire cricket batting record is held by a man who made his debut for the club in 1873, the year that a County Championship was first established, and only ten years after the formation of the County Club. He is Louis Hall, and he carried his bat through a completed innings in a first class fixture for Yorkshire on 14 occasions. He is followed by Geoffrey Boycott (8), Herbert Sutcliffe (5), and Percy Holmes (3). Will Hall's record ever be broken?

Boycott scored 103 centuries for Yorkshire, Sutcliffe 112 and Holmes 60. Louis Hall reached the 100 mark a mere nine times. He was a slow scorer and in only 4 out of the 14 occasions in which he carried his bat did Hall make an unbeaten century.

Louis Hall was born in Batley on 1 November 1852, the youngest of eight children of Thomas and Martha Hall. By the end of the 1850s, Thomas had become a woollen manufacturer. In the 1870s, when Louis was a professional cricketer, his father's firm had three premises and was a significant employer in the town. The main mill was burnt down some time in the 1880s, after which the firm seems then to have gone into speedy oblivion. By then, Louis Hall was one of the leading cricketers of his day.

Louis learnt his cricket at Osborne's School in Batley. In 1871 he joined the newly formed Batley Cricket Club. His Yorkshire debut, in May 1873 at the age of 21, was against Middlesex at the Princes Ground, Harrow. His 37 in the first innings was described in *Wisden* as "a promising batting display that showed careful and good defence." Promise that was not fulfilled. He played nine times in all scoring only 118 runs at an average of 8.42, with that 37 in his very first knock his best score of the season.

Hall dropped out of the county side, returning to club cricket. In 1878 he scored 79 for a Hunslet XVIII against the Australians (demon Spofforth and all), enough for him to be selected against Surrey at the Oval. He played nine games that season and finished second in the Yorkshire averages. By the following season, 1879, he was a regular member of the Yorkshire side and continued to be so until his retirement in 1892.

Hall scored 9,757 runs for Yorkshire in first class matches at an average of 23.28, with nine centuries. As batting averages of this period should almost be doubled for fair comparison with today's batsmen, Hall's figures represent a considerable achievement. He topped the county averages in 1883, scored four hundreds in 1884 and exceeded 1,000 runs in 1887, including his highest score in first class cricket, 160 (out of 590) against Lancashire in 1887 (occupying the crease for a total of 6 hours and 40 minutes) when he and Fred Lee put on 280 for the second wicket.

Batley CC   **Drawing by Sue Brant**

Hall was never capped by England and he will be remembered for his slow scoring. *Wisden* summed up his value in its 1916 obituary, "It cannot be said that he was an attractive bat to watch – he was at times a veritable stonewaller – but in the Yorkshire eleven which included George Ulyett and William Bates, his stubborn defence was of priceless value. In match after match he kept up his wicket while one or other of those brilliant hitters demoralised the bowling."

Louis Hall frequently captained Yorkshire, deputising for Lord Hawke who had been appointed captain in 1883, but did not assume the post on a full-time basis until 1886. Hall was a non-smoker, teetotaller and Methodist lay preacher. It was said that Lord Hawke's task as captain was "to lead a team of nine drunks and a chapel person." This was later changed to a team that "had suffered from the injudicious hospitality of friends." In Lord Hawke's view, "the moral character of my men is of infinitely more importance than their form." In 1897, Bobby Peel was summarily dismissed from the field at Chesterfield, and subsequently from Yorkshire, for being worse the wear for drink. In contrast, Lord Hawke described Louis Hall as a "gentleman professional" adding "higher praise cannot be given."

Hall became chairman of the Yorkshire Cricketers' Benevolent Fund. He remarked, "With regard to old cricketers, I think the county is now in a position which should enable it to prevent the layers of the foundation stones of Yorkshire cricket ending their days in poverty."

When his cricket career was over, Hall became a wool merchant and public servant. He was elected to the Batley Borough Council in 1904 as a Liberal. He was to hold his seat for nine years until failing health forced him to give it up in 1913.

Louis Hall retired to Morecambe, believing that the sea air would be good for his health and died there on 19 November 1915, aged 63 years. At his funeral in Batley, many tributes were paid to his character and achievements. But Louis Hall's lasting, probably everlasting, memorial will be that he carried his bat for Yorkshire on 14 occasions.

Alonzo Drake: All-Round Star
Peter Redding

Few careers have been as short and as sweet as that of ex-Honley star Alonzo Drake. He was 25 before he made his debut for Yorkshire when a combination of the First World War and ill health restricted him to just six seasons. His cricketing career began with Honley in 1906. In 1907 he picked up the Huddersfield League batting prize with an impressive average of 53. He is however, best remembered for being one of the most lethal bowlers around on uncovered pitches.

Establishing himself in the notoriously strong Yorkshire side proved taxing. He made a half-century on his debut in 1909 against Derbyshire and picked up 6 for 34, including a hat trick, in his second game against Middlesex. But, he made only five more appearances that summer.

During the 1911 season he averaged 35 with the bat and picked up 79 wickets at 22.4, in the process forming a deadly all-round alliance with fellow Huddersfield star Wilfred Rhodes. He also made his maiden first

class century against Derbyshire at Chesterfield, scoring 147 not out, his career best score. The highlight with the ball was 6 for 57 in the Roses win over Lancashire at Old Trafford.

In 1912 he picked up 86 wickets as Yorkshire won the County Championship. The 1913 and 1914 seasons were his last. He took 7 for 7 against Somerset and 4 wickets in 4 balls against Derbyshire. His most famous performance came in his penultimate first class game against Somerset with all 10 wickets for 35 runs in the second innings, finishing with 15 wickets in the match.

Throughout his career, Drake remained loyal to Honley, turning out whenever his first class commitments allowed. Sadly 1914 proved to be his final season. Cricket did not resume until 1919, the same year that he died, aged just 34.

Mirfield Collection

Mirfield Beginnings 1862-6
Pat Neal

The Mirfield Cricket Club appears to have been formed some time in 1862. *The Dewsbury District News* published some cricketers' tales in 1904:

> The first field was laid out through the generosity of several local gentlemen who became guarantors for the expenses incurred. Amongst these were Armitage Rhodes, John Topham, John Holmes and James Crowther … John Eyres was the first secretary of the club and he was also stationmaster at Mirfield.

James Firth Crowther owned the maltings of JF & J Crowther Limited and ran a stud farm breeding shire horses. The field, or *enclosure*, was sited at the top north-eastern corner of the Blake Hall estate on the land of Joshua Ingham. It can be found on the corner of the present Crowlees Road and Pinfold Lane and is now covered in houses. The club played on this ground until 1895 when the railway forced a move to Park Bottom (now known as the Memorial Ground).

The Dewsbury Reporter has one reference to Mirfield Cricket Club on 10th August 1862:

The Mirfield Cricket Club versus The Thornhill Lees Church Institute Club – the return match between the above clubs was played on Saturday last, on the ground of the latter, which resulted in an easy victory for the Mirfield Club … The first match, which came off a few weeks ago, was won by Thornhill.

The Dewsbury Reporter dated 9th May 1863 reports on the first Annual General Meeting held on Monday 2nd May:

The members of this club held their first annual meeting last Monday evening in the Towngate School room. Mr R. Denton in the chair. The report was read by the returning secretary, Mr T. Haworth … The expenses during the past year have been heavy, they having purchased a large number of bats, etc and also having had their field levelled and re-laid. There is, however, a small balance in hand. Mr G. Moffatt of Over Hall was voted secretary for the ensuing year. The admission fee has been advanced to 10s.

On 14th May, Mirfield entertained Church Institute Thornhill Lees in a two-innings match. *The Dewsbury Reporter's* account reads:

This match, as advertised in out last issue, came off on Saturday last, on the excellent ground of the Mirfield Club, and attracted a considerable number of spectators. It is the first match of the season for the Church Institute players, and when friends and others heard of the challenge having been sent to the Mirfield gentlemen, they characterised it as a "piece of impudence", and prophesied that they would have to repent of their audacity. The contrast in appearance of the two elevens rather justified such opinions, but the result proved a victory for the Thornhill Lees players who beat their opponents with seven wickets to fall. The bowling of Hill and J. Wilson was very good, as was the batting of Thompson. Smithson's bowling was "too impetuous" and of course did not do much damage.

This may be the first reference to Allen Hill as professional who later played for Yorkshire. In 1877, it's said he took the first wicket and catch in Test cricket when he played for Lillywhite's XI in Melbourne.

G H Hirst of Mirfield 1891
Pat Neal

Cast your mind back 114 years to the year 1891 when Queen Victoria was in her early seventies and nearing the end of her glorious reign. The Conservative Party was in power with the 3rd Marquess of Salisbury the Prime Minister, and the Liberals, under the leadership of William Ewart Gladstone, were in opposition. The Factory Act was passed, changing the minimum age of a child being able to work in a factory from ten to eleven! Horseless carriages still had to have a man walk in front waving a red flag. It was a year when Britain was linked to Europe for the first time by telephone and the first Crufts Dog Show was held.

In sport the first French Tennis Open was staged. The Football League was only three years old. In cricket, Yorkshire played their first ever match at Headingley, entertaining Derbyshire. Surrey won the County Championship with Yorkshire a poor eighth. It was the first year of the Huddersfield Cricket League. In December 1892 WG Grace led the MCC to Australia in where they lost the Ashes 2-1.

In Mirfield, the main event was the Mirfield Colliery Company's new shaft, sunk near the King's Head Inn. This connected with the mine workings in Dark Lane, giving a means of escape in an emergency. Until 1895, it is believed that Mirfield Cricket Club was based at a ground on what is now the corner of Pinfold Lane and Crowlees Road. The London & North Western Railway Company then turned them out by building their new line from Heddon Lodge to Wortley straight through the ground.

George Herbert Hirst had played cricket for his local village, Kirkheaton, before turning professional in 1890 for Elland. In 1891 he travelled over the hill to Mirfield. In his interview for *Cricket: A Weekly Record* in 1893, he tells of his early days in club cricket and how they helped shape his game:

> I went to Elland first, then to Mirfield, and lastly to Huddersfield, where last year and this I have been engaged. Besides cricket, I am very fond of football [rugby], and played as centre three quarter for Mirfield. But I like cricket best. And by joining other clubs I learned something. You know what a lot of good cricket there is in these local clubs of ours; why, nearly all our county players belong to one or more of them and help them in the Saturday matches whenever we can get off, so from time to time I met our best batsmen and bowlers. And I found out that you must suit your bowling to the batsman, and to the state of the wicket as well, and in that way my bowling improved. That's the reason, I suppose, why at last I got into the county eleven, for which I played most of last season.

In 1891 the Census taken in March tells us that George Herbert was living in the area known as New Town in Kirkheaton. He lived with his parents John and Mary Berry, who had eventually married, along with his brother. He was aged 19 and was employed as a cotton dyer. His first game appears to have been at home to Marsden on Saturday 25 April, where he scored 24 runs in a total of 62. Marsden scored 104 for 7 in reply, George Herbert taking three wickets. *The Dewsbury District News* reported on the match, even giving him the wrong initials:

> The Mirfield team are this year strengthened by the presence of JH Hirst who is acting as professional. On Saturday he opened his account with a well earned 24 before Wrigley displaced his stumps.

The paper also gives an insight into the Mirfield club which obviously had been through a tough time:

> English is again included in the team. A few seasons ago he did wonderful work along with E Fleetwood. These two lifted the club a little out of the mire into which it had seemed to have fallen. This year a great gap in Mirfield ranks, owing to the loss the club has sustained by the death of Mr. H Ibberson, a sterling batsman, who played with great confidence and skill. He was of the greatest service to the club. Another player of the best credentials was also absent on Saturday, I mean HC Walker, one of the prettiest bats in the district; his presence gives a great amount of confidence to the players.

The Huddersfield Examiner wrote, "None of them was able to stand against Wrigley's bowling, except GH Hirst, whose 24 was got by some fine hitting."

Mirfield's Move To Park Bottom 1895
Pat Neal

The year 1894 saw the last season at the Mirfield Enclosure at the northeast corner of the Blake Hall Estate. Mirfield were then part of the Spen Valley League playing games against Cleckheaton, Spen Victoria, Staincliffe, Roberttown, Birkenshaw, Scholes Albert Mills, and Heckmondwike. It was poor season on the field. Just 5 wins and 10 losses, ending with defeats to Scholes and Birkenshaw. The *Dewsbury District News* commented on the Scholes game: "The display of the Mirfield eleven was weak and unsatisfactory." Mirfield were bowled out for 29 in reply to Scholes 130 for 7. At Birkenshaw, Mirfield appear to have struggled for a team. The *District News* stated "Mirfield with a weak team and comprising a lot of the Parish Church eleven journeyed to Birkenshaw." They were bowled out for 50 and despite Walker's 5 for 20. Birkenshaw made 52 for 8.

At the end of the season, a report, given by joint secretaries CA Walker and H Haworth, at the Annual General Meeting held at the Black Bull

Hotel on Wednesday 18 December 1895, contained the following: "Owing to the construction of the Heaton Lodge and Wortley Railway; it became necessary at the end of the season 1894, to select a new ground, lay a new cricket pitch, and erect a new pavilion."

The original *enclosure* was on the Blake Hall Estate. Mr Edward Theodore Ingham, owner of Blake Hall, appears to have provided a new field at the bottom of the estate at Park Bottom. This field later became the Memorial Ground after the Great War. The report goes on:

The Committee thought that in doing this they should provide a ground and pavilion worthy of the place, and they were at the outset met most favourably by Mr Ingham, who placed at their disposal a field very suitable for the purpose.

The season's play has had to be conducted under great difficulties. Owing to the unprecedented severity of the winter, the ground could not be got ready for play until the season was well advanced, and the pavilion was not finished until the end of the season. Under these circumstances a successful season could not be looked for, but though there has been a considerable loss on the year's working, still this loss has not been so great as was at one time anticipated.

...the Club has won 9 matches, lost 8 and drawn 5.

...the Committee feel that a good ground and pavilion having been provided, there is every reason to believe that in the future the Club will prosper, and they earnestly appeal to all lovers of Cricket in Mirfield and neighbourhood to make the Club, as it well might be, one of the foremost in the district.

...the Committee, seeing that they were unable to raise the required funds, appealed to Mr.Ingham to assist them. After consideration, he offered (1) to give the Club lease of the ground for 10 years at the present rent with a clause for renewal; (2) to pay further sum of £200 in addition to the £100 already paid by him, and to take over the pavilion as his property, letting the same to the Club free of rent for 7 years and afterwards charging £10 a year rent. In this way, calculating the rent which Mr.Ingham offers to allow, he will have paid £370 which is the actual cost of the construction of the pavilion. The Committee unanimously resolved to accept Mr.Ingham's generous offer and recommend it to the meeting.

Unfortunately, the local newspapers make no reference in 1894 or 1895 to the club having to move grounds due to the railway. Occasionally, there is reference to work being done on the railway as on 24th July 1895 the Dewsbury Reporter commented "a good number of navvies are at work at Northorpe and Battyeford."

The fixture list for 1895 indicates that the club must have pulled out of the Spen Valley League, probably due to the uncertainty with the ground. The season saw matches home and away scheduled with the following clubs: King Cross, Headingley, Scholes, Honley, Dewsbury & Savile 'A', Farnley, Bankfoot, an Huddersfield XI, Eccleshill

and Farnley Iron Works, as well as return games against K Lockwood's XI.

We know from the annual report the team had a better season than in 1894. The first game on the new ground went unreported except for the score, Mirfield scoring 72 with C Halliday top scoring with 13. Honley scored 122 for 7.

The last game of the season on 14 September ended in defeat by three wickets to King Cross, Mirfield making 60. The same week the *Dewsbury Reporter* commented 'the railway cutting is coming on fast.'

Memorable Matches

Wirksworth v All England
Roy Pearce

An All England XI appeared in Wirksworth three times: 1866, 1868 and 1870. William Clarke created the team in 1846 from working class professionals from the Nottingham area. Playing three-day games, they were entertained royally by the local cricketers and their sponsors. Wages were good, usually supplemented by stake money. Wirksworth played with 22 players and included professional bowlers hired for the occasion.

The following are taken from 1866 local press reports:

The wicket which had been prepared was not altogether approved of by the eleven, and at their request it was slightly altered, but not for the better.

The refreshment booths and other temporary erections gave the grounds a very animated appearance, especially when about twelve o'clock the spectators began to pour in, some on foot, some on horse back and others in carriages. The lovely Derbyshire scenery around was most beautiful, and greatly admired by everyone present.

At a quarter past eleven the splendid band of the Matlock Rifle Volunteers marched into the town, playing a quick step. Everybody seemed to know in a moment what band it was, and there was very soon a large crowd of persons gathered round them… prior to marching off home, which they managed to do about nine o'clock. The ground today had a very different appearance as far as the spectators are concerned, there being apparently three or four times as many persons present as there was yesterday. It was thought that no less than from 2,000 to 3,000 persons passed through the gates. Most of the shops in the town were closed today.

The large company of spectators, composed of all classes, was extremely well behaved during the whole of the time, and the greatest interest was felt in the game, as was evinced by the frequent bursts of applause at good play. At the conclusion of the game (6 o'clock) the Eleven posted off to Cromford Station to catch the 7pm train for Manchester, so play was kept up to the very last minute.

This is a staggering attendance, even allowing for some press exaggeration, for a small town with hardly 5,000 people in the area, and indicates the enormous delight in an isolated Victorian community when any entertainment was provided. The 1870 balance sheet was as follows:

Income:
subscriptions [from the sponsors]	£75-6-0
admission (6d)	£37-2-6
booths & stalls	£7-12-6

Expenses:
All England	£65
Professional bowlers	£10-10
Other expenses	£59-16

The club made a profit of £20. 2,895 paid to get in, not quite as many as the press reports suggested, but still an impressive attendance.

All England won two games and the other was drawn. Their team in 1866 included E Stephenson, J Smith, A Sears, T Hayward, W Oscroft, G Parr, J Rowbottom, G Tarrant, RC Tinley, J Jackson, and JC Shaw. A Shaw, (15 wickets in one innings, 26 in the match in 1870), G Pinder and T Emmett, three mighty performers, were selected in the subsequent matches.

Ranjhitsinji, in his Jubilee Book of Cricket, ghost-written by CB Fry, writes that WG Grace, who knew about professionalism, spoke as follows of the All England Team:

The All England Eleven was started by one man and conducted on business principles and while it lived … helped to spread abroad a knowledge of the game … the majority of the players were the best professionals in England and under his leadership were open for engagements anywhere, as long as they obtained their price.

Clarke, owner of the *Trent Bridge Inn*, put his case "I want to play cricket because I like it. It is my profession and may fairly be made as lucrative as possible … The public is interested in cricket and will pay to see it."

Ranji explains "A professional player in former times was entirely the servant of his club and in a servant's position. In Exhibition elevens, he became a free member of a professional team."

(Formed in 1849, Wirksworth is now Wirksworth and Middleton CC)

Elland in the 1870s and 1880s
Rob Light

In the late 1870s and 1880s the rising status and ambition of Elland Cricket Club was reflected in a series of major matches which were played at Hullen Edge. Staging this type of *big match* cricket, against leading touring XI's, had been a common way of attracting prestige for clubs in the district since the 1840s. Leading players came together to form teams which could be hired to play matches against local and district sides of varying numbers. This meant that nearly all the great cricketers of this era could be seen regularly at local cricket grounds each year. Not surprisingly, these matches were the major events of the season.

The 1846 All England XI was the first to tour, playing at Leeds. Regular annual matches were then played by this team and others in Huddersfield, Halifax, Dewsbury, Batley, Todmorden, Bradford and elsewhere in Yorkshire. The most famous of these *big matches* to be held at Elland was the first one, against the 1878 Australian Tourists.

(Elland was formed in 1860 and play in the Huddersfield League)

Early Club Benefactor

Samuel Fielden
Brian Heywood

Eldest son of cotton manufacturer and MP for Oldham John Fielden, Sam developed his passion for cricket at public school. On his return to Todmorden in 1834 he was put in charge of the Waterside Mill, where he gave some of the factory workers time off with pay to play cricket with him on the hillside behind the mill, at Shoebroad Field, Longfield. It was here that Todmorden Cricket Club was formed in 1835.

A fast underhand bowler and decent batsman, Sam was treasurer and ran the club until it disbanded in 1841. In 1849, Sam inherited the Centre Vale estate from his father and immediately re-formed the club. As a shareholder in the Lancashire-Yorkshire Railway and a leading light in local affairs (and national ones in supporting the interests of factory workers), but he was often too busy to play, he remained President of the cricket club, owned the ground and followed the club's fortunes closely. He paid for the Burnley Road wall and the new tea pavilion in time for the prestigious 1874 match between the United North and the United South of England. When this match finished before lunch on the

third day, the club faced a financial loss and Sam persuaded the players, including WG Grace, to stay and play a one innings match in the afternoon.

Incensed by younger members breaking into the pavilion in 1875, and having little faith in the competence of the committee, Sam insisted on an increase in membership fees to create a smaller and more exclusive membership. He also put the club on annual probation. When members voted to reduce the age and fees for membership at the AGM of 1885, they were refused use of the ground unless they reversed the decision, and Sam did not confirm the ground's availability until April 1886.

For all his threats, it is doubtful if Sam would have closed the ground as he had a genuine love of cricket.

(Cricket has been played at Todmorden since 1835. The club have been at their current ground, Centre Vale, since 1839 and joined the Lancashire League in 1897)

Miscellany

Was Shaw A Shamateur?
William Marshall

In the 1897 Halifax Parish Cup, Southowram St Anne's lost to Shelf in the preliminary round, thanks largely to a score of 56 plundered by an all-rounder named J Shaw, who won the round's batting prize for his impressive score. But Southowram officials smelt a rat. They were convinced that Shaw was a professional, playing in contravention of the rules of the Parish Cup. On June 4, 1897, a special meeting of the Parish Cup Committee was called. It was alleged that Shaw had received his travelling expenses and that was enough to brand him a *pro*.

A Shelf representative owned up, but stated that Shaw had received only his bus and railway fares and not a penny more. Shaw was "not a professional in any shape or form" said Mr Hind, the Shelf President. The club's books were examined and the Committee decided that Southowram had not produced sufficient evidence to prove Shaw's professionalism and the case was dismissed.

Whether or not he was a *pro*, Shaw was certainly a fine player. In the next round of the Cup he won the batting prize again, scoring 70 for Shelf against Luddenden Foot. And in the semi-final he won the bowling prize, with a haul of 5 for 30 against Illingworth.

2 - Twentieth Century
Part 1 1900-49

Drawing by Clive Hetherington

Survival and Growth

A Scorebox from Nottingham: Part I
Rob Hardie

Despite finding a permanent home and having a field to play their home matches on, it took a further 20 years before Slaithwaite began to develop the land around the playing surface. 1901 saw the first stone of the clubhouse laid, with the bowling green and cricket pavilion following seven years later in 1908.

The scorer kept tally on his own. To keep up with other clubs, Slaithwaite decided they needed a scorebox. Thus, in 1945, instead of building their own, they shipped one in from the East Midlands. This, the first scorebox to appear at Hill Top, was given to the club as a present. Sir Julian Cahn presented the box to the family of former club President, Mr James Gartside. This was then given to Slaithwaite in his honour and to preserve his memory. The box's previous home was Sir Julian's's own private cricket ground in Nottingham.

The building was presented formally on the 11 August 1945 in front of local and county cricket officials and was said to be "a credit to any cricket ground in the country" by Huddersfield District Cricket League President, Mr WH Bolt. During his time at the club, West Indian professional Edwin St. Hill kept the box running smoothly.

(Slaithwaite was established as Slaithwaite St James in 1873, changing to Slaithwaite Cricket and Athletic Club in 1877. The club plays in the Huddersfield League)

Bats, Balls and Biscuits
Martin Bishop

During, and following, the horrors of the First World War, the Reading Biscuit Factory, along with many other organisations, reeled under its losses and the fundamental changes that the war years imposed.

Prior to the outbreak of war, the Biscuit Factory had traditionally employed men and boys. Of a working population of approximately 5000 in the factory, 1833 were to serve in the armed forces. The vacancies caused by this exodus of men were filled by employing women to a level previously unknown in the factory.

Of the 1833 who served, 145 were never to return. By June 1919, 832 of the survivors had returned to Reading. The rest returned over the following months and all but ten returned to the factory.

In mid-May 1919 the post-war cricket season stuttered into action. The *Reading Chronicle* of the 16 May 1919, in a special article, launched the post-war Reading Biscuit Factory Recreation Club and outlined it's planned activities for 1919. The headline detailed the acquisition of the former Reading and District Amateur Sports Club ground, the County Cricket ground, at Kensington Road in West Reading, for use by Recreation Club members.

Enthusiasm for a return to the full range of activities offered by the Recreation Club was high, but with the loss of some former *star artists*, there was obviously great sadness and apprehension.

The Recreation Club had a new General Secretary, Captain DG Leadley, formerly of the Royal Fusiliers, who was to prove a great addition to the playing strength of the cricket club. Captain Leadley produced an excellent fixture card for the cricket club which ran three teams for the 1919 season (an understandable reduction from the five teams of the 1914 season). Of the 46 scheduled fixtures, only three were planned to

Martin Bishop

be played away from the club's home *enclosures*, an indication that the Recreation Club Ground at Kings Meadow and the Kensington Road Ground had been maintained to a reasonable level during the war years. Other Club or Council grounds had probably not received the same attention and the recovery of cricket activity for those playing on these grounds was to take a little longer.

(Cricket began on Sundays in the 1860s between teams such as Sugar Wafers and Invoice Room. The club lost its independence following a merger with Purley in 1984)

SBCI 1934-46
Brian Heywood

The period between 1934 and 1946 was a traumatic time. Prior to 1934 the cricket club was funded by nominal match fees and a cut it received from the Institute's fund raising activities. The cricketers contributed to events such as bazaars as they were primarily members of the Institute, and not just the cricket club.

Part of the club's commitment was to pay an annual rent to the Institute's Management Committee. These payments had, apparently, lapsed and in 1934 the Committee adopted the resolution "that the Cricket Section be not allowed use of the playing field unless they can guarantee their rent."

The Cricket Section replied:

We regret that the Management Committee have seen reason to censure that section ... the Cricket Section has always been more or less subsidised from the Institute funds, further, up to 1934, the Cricket Section were not allowed to organise events for the purpose of raising funds, owing to the existence of a Social Committee.

Although subsidised by Institute events such as jumble sales and the Christmas Club, the Cricket Section needed more funds. The cricket committee requested a 12 month abeyance before any action was taken and embarked on frantic fund-raising preparations. Motivated by survival, the Cricket Section began to adopt the methods of clubs with much greater manpower, financial turnover and security.

Bi-annual Whist Drive and Dances were organised for February and October, membership cards and fixture lists were printed, their costs covered by advertisements. Old members and friends were cajoled to renew their interest in the club and *prominent gentlemen* were approached to become vice-presidents, though the club had only one of these, a local vicar, by 1937.

The first Whist Drive and Dance was held at the Victoria Assembly Rooms on 2 February 1935. 200 tickets and 50 window bills were printed and the 5-piece New Astoria Band booked at a cost of 50 shillings. The profit of £2 14s 6d made it the most successful of the new initiatives.

By 1936 the annual rent for the field was £8 8s. The club's financial struggles were highlighted the following winter when the pitch was returfed "using sods from our own field" and bitter objections were raised to an invoice for 13 hours rolling over two days when the committee had only requested eight hours rolling on one day. To pay for this work, the club embarked on a *mile of pennies* scheme and 1000 envelopes were printed and distributed around the district.

The war deeply hurt SBCI. Continuity disintegrated. There were no committee meetings between March 1940 and September 1941, at which point the club ceased to function and the ground fell into five years of neglect.

In post-war Britain, symbolising a return to normality, team sports, particularly football and cricket, were embraced by communities as never before. The cricket club was already underway when the Institute re-started its other activities at an Extraordinary General Meeting on 26 June 1946. With the Reverend RW Scott presiding, billiards, snooker, table tennis, dominoes, draughts and cards were re-started.

By the end of the 1950s, support for cricket was dwindling and the church was floundering. The advent of counter-attractions, particularly the car and television, eroded the tradition of Sunday as a day for family and worship. In 1960, the cricket club's secretary, Walter Birkby, and treasurer, Fred Bates, were instructed "to act for the Institute" during a period when the rest of the church organisation, including all the indoor activities, shut down.

Today the letters SBCI are synonymous with cricket. The club has outlived its parent body (the Institute's social club) and, with the opening of its £228, 000 pavilion in 1999, is utterly transformed from the vulnerable adolescent of 70 years ago. The hardy band who nurtured the club through its acute growing pains of the 1930s and 1940s would be delighted and amazed.

The ground, although controlled by the cricket club, is still held by church trustees and, in a tradition dating to the early days, the Vicar of Christ Church is still the cricket club's President.

Professionals

Wilf Barber, Brighouse and England
Matt Carswell

Wilf Barber was born in Cleckheaton, Yorkshire, on 18 April 1901. He was a professional for Yorkshire between 1926 and 1947 and also represented England in two Tests in 1935 against South Africa. During his time at Yorkshire he won the County Championship eight times, scoring a total of 16,402 runs in 373 first-class matches.

Barber achieved a career average of 34.38 runs and made 29 career centuries, 27 of which were for Yorkshire. His most successful season was in 1935 when he made 2,147 at an average of 42.09. This was one of eight seasons when he exceeded 1,000 runs. In 1935, he hit a personal highest score of 285 against Surrey at Bramall Lane, Sheffield.

His first Test match was at Headingley against South Africa where he made a total of 38 runs in his two innings. The match was eventually drawn. Although not known for his bowling, he tops the all-time Test Match bowling lists! He took one wicket from two balls in this Test. His second and final Test was the fourth Test of the same series at Old Trafford. This time he made a total of 45 runs and this match was also drawn. He toured

Australasia with the MCC in 1935/36, making 91 against Queensland at Brisbane. In New Zealand he scored 365 runs in four matches including 116 against Canterbury.

The highest partnership Barber took part in (still a Yorkshire record to this day) was with Maurice Leyland against Middlesex at Sheffield in 1932. In four and a half hours they made a total of 346 with Barber making 162 and Leyland hitting 189, even with the help of a runner!

After he retired, Barber became groundsman and coach at a school in Harrogate. He died in a Bradford hospital on 10 September, 1967, aged 66.

Learie Constantine and Edwin St Hill
Mark Edmonds

Edwin St. Hill is regarded as one of Slaithwaite's greatest players and the first black player to represent a side in the Huddersfield League. The man behind this move was the great West Indian all-rounder Sir Learie Nicholas Constantine, known later as Baron Constantine.

On 20 June 1933, Constantine was the main attraction at a friendly between Slaithwaite and a team selected by then Paddock captain Herbert Robinson. The Robinson XI comprised the best players from the Bradford League, while Slaithwaite called upon the services of Constantine and St Hill as well as players from Huddersfield and Thongsbridge.

Constantine was a right-hand batsman who could bowl both medium and fast. He made 18 Test appearances for the Windies, finishing with a batting average of 19.24. He also took 58 wickets at an average of 30.10. He made five first class hundreds with career best bowling figures of 8 for 38. He was named one of Wisden's five Cricketers of the Year in 1940. In 1945, he was awarded the MBE for services to the game and was knighted in 1962.

St Hill was big news when he came to Slaithwaite, with a crowd of between 4,000 and 5,000 coming to the ground to see the all-rounder in action. All the attention he received obviously had an effect, as he signed for the club later that season.

To put the signing of St Hill into perspective, the all-rounder was paid £240 for the season and granted a benefit match. Although this was a lot of money in the thirties, today it is less than the average weekly wage! The £240 was money well spent though, as, in his first season, the club received over £500 in gate money, more than paying for both St. Hill's services and the everyday running of the club.

(St Hill was a professional at Slaithwaite in 1934 and 1945)

Eddie Leadbeater: Leg-Spin Wizard
David Brenchley

Born in Lockwood in 1927, Eddie Leadbeater started and finished his cricketing career with Almondbury. In between, he represented Yorkshire and Warwickshire as well as gaining two Test caps.

Leadbeater won the Sykes Cup twice with Almondbury. First in 1943 when he took an impressive 6 for 16, and then 19 years later as a professional, when he scored 105.

With Yorkshire between 1949 and 1956, he joined Warwickshire for 1957 and 1958, possibly as a replacement for leg-spinner Eric Hollies.

His Test career was unimpressive. He was a surprise call-up for the tour of India where he took just one wicket (his figures were 1 for 100 off 25.1 overs), held one catch and scored 2 runs. His second Test was his last. He scored 36 before taking 1 for 118 from 23 overs. His Test bowling average is thus 109 at an economy rate of 4.52.

Leadbeater is a rarity as an England Test cricketer. He played for his country without being awarded a county cap.

Although he wasn't renowned for his batting (he averaged just 15.17) he made three 50s and his highest score for Yorkshire was 91. While playing for Warwickshire against Glamorgan in his last year, though, he came in as a night-watchman and hit 116, sharing a second-wicket stand of 206 with Fred Gardner.

His bowling was more impressive. At the end of a nine-year career his economy was 2.87 and he averaged 27.49. In his greatest match, he took 8 for 83 as Yorkshire beat Hampshire by more than an innings.

Cumberworth Partnership

Friend Allsop
Andrew Pearson

The name of Friend Allsop is closely linked with the Cumberworth community and, in particular, with its cricket club. Apart from a short spell with Shepley when they were in the Huddersfield Central League, most of his playing days were spent with his village club.

Since 1953 his name has been associated with the Allsop Cup, presented in his memory by Cumberworth United, for the winners of the Central League's first team knock out competition. The citation on the cup states that the intention was "to perpetuate the memory of a great sportsman."

Reflections on him are made in *A History of Cumberworth: Camp of the Cumbrians*, written by A Tarbatt and published in 1980. His prowess at cricket was evident from an early age because it is reported that, when at Denby Dale Council School: "Friend made his fifties when other boys were pleased to make their tens." From his earliest years he was able to play strokes all round the wicket and it was stated that his defence was like a barn door. Pulls and swings to leg came easily to him and the hitting of sixes when the opportunity arose seemed effortless.

He was very much a team player and sympathetic to those with lesser skills. Sacrificing his wicket to let others have a knock was not unknown when the situation in the game permitted it. The decision of the umpire was never questioned.

Drawing by Sue Brant

In 1933 he totalled 1070 runs at an average of 59.40, followed by 1015 runs in 1934, averaging 67.66 per innings. Whilst building his own house, it was alleged that the regular collections from his batting feats were of great help to settle his bills.

In the book by A Tarbatt, we learn he was very sensitive to injustice of any kind and often felt despair at how others sometimes conducted themselves. He was "a keen nature and garden lover", attended WEA classes and was a member of a local male voice choir. It is also recorded that he was an accomplished billiards player.

Ken Smith
Andrew Pearson

Born in 1919, Ken Smith is one of the oldest surviving former playing members of the club. He joined as a junior in 1932. In the senior team he recalls opening the batting with Friend Allsop. Large numbers would come to watch this prolific village batsman. In one game against Penistone Netherfield he ran Friend out. He was close to tears and the spectators were disappointed at not seeing Friend bat for longer.

In his early years travel in the First and Second team was by a waggonette owned by Mr H Roberts. After being taken to the heights of Cartworth Moor on one occasion, the driver informed the team that his return might be delayed as he was involved in hay making. The game finished and the team repaired to the nearby *Rising Sun*, destroyed by fire in the mid 1970s. Long hours passed and the drink flowed more and more freely, and when the waggonette eventually made its appearance the Cumberworth players were certainly in a boisterous mood as they climbed aboard for the journey home.

He remembers the arrival of the goods vans in 1948. Cecil Auckland helped manoeuvre them into position. Unfortunately, at a key moment, a couple of fingers were caught underneath. Luckily, no permanent damage was done but Cumberworth was without a key bowler for a week or two whilst he recovered.

The outfield was cut manually before the advent of mechanical mowing. Games of nipsy, a close relative of knur and spell, were played in the 1930s, where the object was to strike a *pig* or small, hard ball, perhaps the size of a large marble, as far as possible. Casual competitions took place between men in the village.

He regarded near neighbours Denby Dale as the club's greatest rivals and he always enjoyed visits to Thurstonland and Skelmanthorpe.

His daughter reminded him of losing a few teeth from his days keeping wicket. He never made a century but had two scores in the nineties, one of them at Penistone. Only rarely was he called upon to bowl. A game at Clayton West explains why. Cumberworth were up against it and, perhaps in desperation, the captain invited him to have a go. The batsman, Percy Bedford, was in full flow and his two overs saw the ball disappear to all areas of the ground. With a wry smile, he said that he was hardly ever asked to perform again.

He played his last game in 1973.

(Cumberworth United was formed in 1876 and currently plays in the Huddersfield Central League)

Benefactor

Charlie Mitchell
Toby Lock

Charlie Mitchell was a player and benefactor for Thurstonland Cricket Club. Charlie owned a local motor engineering company which was founded at the turn of the century.

He was thought to be a little too influential when it came to picking the team, and it was thus dubbed *Mitchell's Team*. One of few vehicle owners with his own business, he was persuasive in attracting new players. Many members of the 1906 Thurstonland side were not even from the area. William Henry Potter was from Brockholes, Ted Pontefract from Huddersfield, Joe Haley hailed from Holmfirth and Harold Pontefract was a Honley boy. Haley was the club's top scorer for three straight years between 1911 and 1913.

The most spectacular player in *Mitchell's Team* was however, a young spin bowler called John Hall, who travelled all the way from Goole. Working on the railways, Hall would meet Mitchell at the railway station and get a lift the rest of the way. Allegedly, Hall's bag was always full of smuggled tobacco from the docks in Goole, which he sold in the village!

Mitchell employed Frank Lee, a great all-rounder who often had a lot of money in his pocket (he once gave a scorer 20 sovereigns to take care of during a game), as well as using teammate Albert Gill to do joinery work for the business.

He entered hill climbing events over Holme Moss. In 1921 Charlie raced his Hutton *Four-Inch* against land speed record holder, Sir Malcolm Campbell's Peugeot, and came out as winner. Whispers around the area, though, claimed that Charlie had *doctored* the course in order to beat Campbell. Charlie also aided world heavyweight boxing champion Jack Johnson when his car broke down. It is still unknown as to why Johnson was even in the area!

(Formed in 1874, Thurstonland plays in Huddersfield's Central League)

Not So Serious

It pays to ask first
Allan Stuttard

Walter Parkinson, Walsden's old fashioned Chairman, kept a tight rein on the club purse strings. He never believed in paying for a job to be done when he could twist members to do it for *nowt*. He straightened bent nails, recycled wood and even bottled the black slime that oozed from the club's grass pit to sell as wonder fertiliser at 6d a time. He guarded the gate on match days with an eagle eye and made sure no one sneaked in.

My favourite Walter story was when Walsden played Milnrow on 28 May 1949. As there was no Sunday cricket in those days, matches were played over two evenings, starting at 6.00 pm. Milnrow were top of the league and Walsden, without a win all season, were entrenched in bottom position. The bus from Milnrow pulled in at 6.45 pm carrying 62 supporters. There was no Health & Safety then. The entrance to the ground was over a rickety wooden bridge with room for only one person at a time and Walt was on the gate. 62 visitors proceeded to cross the bridge one at a time, past Walter who charged 6d per person.

Milnrow were 20 for 1 as the first one entered the ground. When the last one got in, at 6.50 pm, they were 26 for 1. He asked whether the low score was due to the wicket doing a bit or had they started late?

"No," said Walter, "you only need 2 to win. Walsden batted first and your *pro,* George Tribe, took 8 for 12 in half an hour, and he's 24 not out."

This match was recorded as the shortest match in the history of the league. George Tribe's 8 wickets came off just 26 balls and he hit three 4s and two 6s in his 24.

Walt said, "I did not tell them or else they would never have paid to get in."

Miscellany

My Grandfather and Golcar
Jane Crane

My grandfather, Mark Gledhill, played for Micklehurst, Saddleworth, when he was 22. My father has just given me a beautiful gold medal dated 1923, and stamped on the back is "Winners of Saddleworth and District League. M. Gledhill". Later he played for Golcar for many years, as he lived opposite the cricket ground in Swallow Lane.

A few years ago, I came up from Poole to Golcar to see the old house and I visited the cricket ground and was able to speak to the club manager. He introduced me to a wonderful old man who remembered my grandfather and my uncle Ian Gledhill, who also played for the team, and told me some funny stories. I remember my grandfather walking me over to the ground as a child, to watch cricket matches on my visits to Golcar with my family.

My father gave me some huge old cricket pads some years ago, and I think these must also have been my grandfather's. I shall always keep them, although I haven't a clue what to do with them! Sentimental value, I suppose!

(Micklehurst, based in Mossley near Stalybridge, were formed in 1890. They joined the Saddleworth and District League in 1900 and the Huddersfield League in 2005)

Cricket Comes
Colin Shakespeare

At the sea's edge, where the land begins,
On smooth, sea-drained sand
A father is bowling to his son;
Family and friends field
And on the breeze the game starts to swing.
Cricket comes, collects its followers
And carries them through the summer,
And omens hoped the game may bring
No one can tell until it ends, or
The spin of a coin and how it lands.
Cricket needs its variations;
Its ups and downs, its fast and slow,
As this land flows in humps and hollows
Towards the horizon's boundary
Where the Pennines meet the sky.
On a scattering of grounds
Play sets the summer free;
It is as if someone above had sprinkled seed
And where it fell cricket grounds grew
To make each summer fresh, each summer, new.

The Round Hill of Rastrick
Mark Whitcombe

The round hill at Rastrick is a bizarre landmark that dominates the cricket club. It is more like a mound and the shape is its main asset, small enough to be admired without being daunting. Directly below it sits the outfield. At the point where it begins to incline, a row of benches has been placed for a good view of the wicket. The green slope then gently rises up towards a symmetrical line of pink flowery bushes halfway. On towards the peak and a top devoid of grass. It is bald. One can only imagine what it looks like in winter. No colour. Just a round grey knoll waiting for Spring and the coming of cricket.

This hill is not just a hill. It is a stand. The Round Hill Stand. Unique.

(Rastrick was formed in 1863 and plays in the Huddersfield League)

Memories of Lascelles Hall 1946-1949
Tony Hutton

I lived in Lascelles Hall village for three years from the Autumn of 1946 to Autumn 1949. At the age of nine it was a considerable upheaval for someone who had been born in Leeds. My father bought a new red brick *semi* on Lascelles Hall Road, alongside the public footpath which went steeply downhill to Waterloo. There were amazing views from my bedroom window of Huddersfield, Castle Hill and the Pennine moors beyond. We were next door to the *Shirt Neck Club*, the scene of a violent murder. I was unaware of that at the time.

I went to Lepton Junior School which was almost in Fenay Bridge, next door to the brickworks, which was then serviced by the Kirkburton railway branch line, with a siding across the road into the brickworks, which we crossed on the way to school.

I soon became a regular at Lascelles Hall cricket ground, spending the summer holidays on the outfield with a bat and tennis ball, with my friends or my cousin who came to stay. I played my first organized game of cricket on the ground. Our school team (under 11s) played another local school on the very far edge of the square. I think the headmaster arranged the game with a member of the committee who had failed to notify the groundsman. A considerable altercation took place, with 22 young boys on tenterhooks as to whether they could play. All was however resolved amicably in the end. As the keenest cricketer I was made captain and kept wicket in a large polo necked white sweater.

The players I remember most from that period were Harry Webster, who I think was the village plumber; Frank Whittle, the wicketkeeper; and most of all, the professional who arrived in 1948, John Whitehead, who was reputed to be the fastest bowler in England.

Whitehead arrived mid-season when the original professional, Entwhistle, was injured. He immediately took wickets galore and bowled the Hall to the Sykes Cup final. I remember going on the bus to the semi final at Holmfirth. Whitehead bowled out Hall Bower for just 50 taking 9 for 15 on debut. This caused uproar among Huddersfield League clubs. Protests were made about employing such a star player half way through a season. The dispute was settled in the Hall's favour two weeks later. Meanwhile, Whitehead took 5 for 17 to dismiss Slaithwaite for 95, Hall winning by 9 wickets.

Hall went on to play Meltham in what turned out to be a three day final at Fartown over the August Bank Holiday weekend. The game started on Saturday in front of a crowd of 6,000 people. Meltham made 153-3 when their innings was suspended and Hall made 120 for 3 in reply when bad light stopped play. Whitehead scored 48.

The game resumed on Bank Holiday Monday, when unfortunately for the Hall, Whitehead was required for Yorkshire Colts. Without him, Meltham piled up a huge score of 330 all out and the Hall were 186 for 7 at the close of play. Only a few overs were required on the Tuesday. Hall were all out for 199 and Meltham won the Sykes Cup by 131 runs.

The following week Whitehead took a hat-trick in a victory over Almondbury, but then they lost again to Huddersfield, mainly due to former Yorkshire player Horace Fisher, the archetypal league professional. He took 8 for 43 and scored 61 not out.

The following year, when available, Whitehead continued with Hall. He also took 14 wickets for the Yorkshire first XI, his most notable performance coming against Derbyshire at Park Avenue when he dismissed four of the first five batsmen on the opening day, reducing Derbyshire to 14 for 4 and then 41 for 5. Yorkshire won comfortably. Unfortunately for Whitehead, his appearance coincided with that of a certain FS Trueman, which was probably why he eventually left for Worcestershire.

My other abiding memory of Whitehead was his long run. He went back almost to the boundary edge where we sat at the Gawthorpe end of the ground. It is hard to say, so many years on, how fast he really was in today's terms.

Sadly, in the Autumn of 1949 my dad got another promotion and we were off to Birmingham. Although I watched both Warwickshire and Worcestershire and played club cricket in the Midlands, I was always staunchly Yorkshire. It took me 20 years to get back to see cricket at Lascelles Hall when Yorkshire played there in benefit games in the 1970s.

There was then another long gap before my next visit in the summer of 2008 when Huddersfield New College played the M.C.C. It was an excellent day in every way, with a lot of cricketing friends in attendance.

During the lunch interval I explored my old haunts. The ground has an improved pavilion, with lots of interesting memorabilia, a new scoreboard and groundsman's equipment store. The wall along the pavilion side of the ground used to be much higher and all the old men sat on benches underneath the wall to avoid the prevailing winds.

The view across the ground to Kirkheaton remains and you can still see the ground on which Hirst and Rhodes learned to play. Lascelles Hall also produced so many great players. It will remain forever in my memories as the very cradle of Yorkshire cricket.

(Established in 1825, Lascelles Hall, the oldest club in the Kirklees area, plays in the Huddersfield League)

Denby's Era in the Penistone League
David Galley

In the late 1940s and early 1950s Denby played in the Penistone League. My uncle was an umpire for Beevor Sports (a Barnsley works team) who were also members of that league. As a young boy I used to go with him to matches and as far as I am aware, no other club from Kirklees was a member of the league.

In 1963 I was a member of the Huddersfield Hospitals cricket team that participated in the Holme Valley Works League. I think we won the league and finished runners up in the cup or vice versa. I believe that I still have my individual trophies hidden away in our garage. We played our home games at Honley.

(Denby was founded in the early 1900s as Denby United. It disbanded in 1958)

Formerly the Huddersfield Royal Infimary, now the Technical College

Interlude - I
The Final that Took Weeks and Weekes
The Early Rounds
Allan Stuttard

In 1955 I joined Walsden Cricket Club, a small village club in Todmorden who played in the Central Lancashire League, the only Yorkshire club to do so. In those days, Walsden was very parochial and hadn't many players from outside the area. I believe, when I made my debut, someone asked, "Who is this then?"

"It's Stuttard from Tod?"

"Is he any good?"

"Don't know, but his mother went to Walsden Chapel, so he must be alright."

It was like batting in a sea of chocolate as the smell from the nearby Rowntree Cocoa factory permeated the air all day.

I was soon made to feel at home and I was introduced to my fellow players, one of whom was Jimmy Wilkinson, Man of the Match in the 1954 Wood Cup Final. This surprised me because, according to the scoresheet, he only scored 17 and didn't bowl or take a catch. I soon found out why and this is the story. Hard to believe but it's true.

In 1954, Walsden were struggling in the lower reaches of the league and had a professional slow left arm bowler from Yorkshire County called Ronnie Wood (brother of Barrie Wood of Lancashire and England). When the draw for the Wood Cup was made, Walsden got a bye; the first time they had got past the first round for many years. They were drawn away at deadly rivals Littleborough for the second round, and a few days prior to the match Ronnie was called up to Yorkshire to replace Johnny Wardle who was injured. A deputy pro had to be found but money was short. So the Chairman and *Wilty*, a local businessman, were asked to cough up. SP Gupte and Vino Mankad were first and second choices but were not available. However, Walsden managed to secure a young West Indian who was with nearby Bacup, and in a thriller, he scored 78 and took 4 for 45. Final scores: Walsden 230, Littleborough 178.

The club was now in the semi-final and drawn away yet again at Milnrow, and Wardle was still injured. The Chairman and *Wilty* were prevailed upon once more. The Chairman asked, "How good is this West Indian, and by the way, what is he called?"

"Not bad," came the reply, "and his name is Everton Weekes."

(Walsden was formed in 1870 and play in the Central Lancashire League)

Slaithwaite

3 - Twentieth Century
Part 2 1950-99

Drawing by Clive Hetherington

Beginnings

Almondbury Casuals 1949-1969
What was the Point of Setting Up a Friendly Cricket Team?
David Walker

In 2006, I was the only friendly cricket representative at an evening class run by Peter Davies and Rob Light from The University of Huddersfield. As my fellow students were die-hard league men or full-time cricket watchers, I asked myself "What is the point of friendly cricket?" This article is a brief answer relevant to the Almondbury Casuals of the 1950s and 1960s.

The post-war preoccupations in cricket have been covered by Derek Birley (2000) in *A Social History of English Cricket* (London: Aurum Press). Briefly, an elite administration faced backwards to the golden age of the gifted amateur as opposed to progressive elements in league cricket and some of the counties who recognised that cricket needed to be more business orientated. Playing became a career option. Interest in results and statistics increased, perhaps at the expense of elegant playing standards. The two sides also differed on access to the game. In the 1950s only 20% of boys, in public and grammar schools, were playing cricket. The elite wanted to retain this exclusiveness to prevent "denaturing" the game. On the other hand, many new clubs started up, for example in villages and companies. Coaching began. The Playing Field Association and English Schools Cricket were formed and overall access to cricket expanded.

A *Casuals* team had played informally from 1949. On 23rd October 1951 a meeting was convened by four of the players to discuss the proposal "that next Summer the Almondbury Casuals should become a small cricket club and should be put on a more organised basis." The minutes record that membership would be a limited to 25, though others might be invited if they were short of players. The four founders were to rotate the captaincy. A local cricket club was to be hired for home games and it was not the intention to seek ambitious fixtures. The opposition for that first season included other friendly teams from West Yorkshire and scratch sides put out by the local rugby and amateur soccer clubs. The headmaster of the local grammar school (King James, Almondbury) became one of the first invitees when approached about use of the school practice nets.

The following quotes, taken from *Cricket in Perspective 1* (1987), compiled by JB Netherwood, illustrate the general feelings as to why the *Casuals* were formed:

> The basic idea was to form a team of cricket lovers…Sunday was the chosen day, when wives, fiancees and girl friends could all join together for a 'happy, convivial and social afternoon/evening together.'
>
> Guy Overton (Chairman 1961-1964)

> As a keen but most unaccomplished player, where else could one have joined a club where one was picked to play for availability rather than capability.
>
> JB Netherwood (Chairman 1969-76)

Again using quotes, there is less agreement as to how the game was played:

> Whoever won the toss, the opposition would bat first…the match would not be over before we could partake of the lovely tea the girls provided…'stumps' were up at 6.50pm to enable us to the pub in time for Sunday opening at 7.00pm.
>
> Guy Overton

> We are endebted to Billy Bolt, Alan Priestley, Jack Taylor and others whose standards are much above average but were happy to play with the *Casuals* and accept with philosophical tolerance the catches put down by supporting fieldsmen.
>
> JB Netherwood

The committee agreed with…JB Netherwood that no member should be consistently placed very low in the batting order with the possibility of missing a 'knock' on several occasions.

Casuals' committee minutes, 1959

It was decided to use the winter shed for practice on the five Sundays March 29th to April 26th inclusive. The secretary was instructed to make the necessary arrangements.

Casuals' committee minutes, 1953

Bill Crossland, the current chairman, has compiled the *Casuals'* statistics. There are three bowlers and three batters from this early era in the top 10. All played league cricket before or after their time with the *Casuals*. The headmaster's son was one, opening the bowling at the age of 14.

The early *Casuals* appear amiable duffers, turning out for the fun of it. Being good at cricket was not a requirement. Some might say they did not take the game seriously enough, perhaps a touch of middle class shyness about growing professionalism in sport. Others might say this was a smokescreen behind which there was serious intent if not always the talent. Anyone watching would have recognised a formal game of cricket: whites, umpires, scorer. Winter nets were provided, weaker cricketers were put down the batting order and league players appeared in the 1960s, all suggesting performance and a result were also relatively important.

What was the point of setting up a friendly cricket team? It widened access to the game of cricket, especially to non-cricketers, youngsters and league men who enjoyed a social game on Sundays.

Queen's Road Muslims 1974-1979
Peter Davies

In June 1974, the Pakistani cricket squad landed on British shores for their fifth tour. Led by Intikhab Alam, they played three Test matches against England, and all three were drawn. Nevertheless, the tour was a great triumph. The Pakistanis were undefeated in their 22 tour matches and won both the one day internationals. The Pakistan squad included players of great pedigree, including Imran Khan, Asif Masood, Sarfraz Nawaz, Asif Iqbal and Sadiq and Mushtaq Mohammad. Four players averaged 50 or more with the bat: Wasim Raja (54.00), Zaheer Abbas (51.31), Shafiq Ahmed (50.11) and Majid Khan (50.00).

Imran, who joined the tour late due to study commitments at Oxford, was in no doubt that it was a path-break-ing tour. In his autobiography, *Imran*, he writes, "We finished the trip un-beaten and I am sure that one of the reasons was that we had toughened up in recent years and were more used to the pressures and tensions of test cricket." Peter Wynne-Thomas in *The Complete History of Cricket Tours at Home and Abroad* argues that this was "the strongest Pakistani side ever to tour England." For the Pakistani community in Britain, the class of '74 were heroes.

At the same time, in the back streets of Halifax, a group of young Asian kids were hanging around street corners wondering what to do. They watched the Test series on television and had seen in Intikhab, Imran and Company Asian sporting idols to emulate. So they wandered down Queen's Road and painted some wickets on an unsuspecting Walsh Street wall. The team that would eventually be known as Queen's Road Muslims had been born. Najabat, one of the co-founders of the team, comments, "The Pakistan side of 1974 were a big influence."

In the very early days, the team was known simply as Queen's Road. The word Muslims was added in 1979 to enhance the identity of the side. It should not be assumed that the team is an overtly religious one. "No," says Najabat, a deft lower-order batsman, "we are not linked to any mosque or any other organisation, though most of us are practising Muslims." He explains that the extra identity is not relevant now. "The team has established itself and the name has just stuck. But really, the philosophy of the side is simple. We just want to give local Asian guys an opportunity to play. Today, for example, several of my nephews play for the side. The name will endure, even though it's not that important anymore."

Queen's Road Tavern

Lest we run away with the impression that QRM is an *exclusive* team, we should note the impact of charismatic West Indian, Copie James. An explosive all-rounder, James was a fixture in the QRM side in the early and mid 1980s. He brought a dash of charisma and acquired a cult reputation. His case is exemplary. It demonstrates the inclusive attitude of QRM and the unique spirit of the club. This is something that current skipper Safdar Hussain is extremely conscious of "Yes, there is an excellent team spirit, and there always has been. Opposition sides respect us; some respect us so much that they lose the game before they arrive at our ground. They hear our name and they do get very fearful. We're also a very open club."

In one season in the late 1970s, QRM played Exley, another local cricket team, 25 times, and won 22 of the encounters! They also played against school sides; they would simply ring up a school, or a teacher, or a contact they had, and spontaneously arrange a fixture. Other teams provided opposition as well: George Lumb, Kashmir, United Biscuits and a team from Elland. Mainly, it was mill and factory sides who gave QRM a game, and they would have to travel by bus to Dewsbury, Elland, Huddersfield or Bradford.

They would play anyone anywhere, and any amount of times. Safdar has been a regular in the side since 1976, "I helped to form the club and I've played non-stop for 28 years. We were just a group of young lads, some who had just left school. None of us owned cars so we had to walk miles and miles with bags of cricket kit. We got very tired!" Ex-Second XI captain Najabat also looks back on these years with a smile on his face, "They were great days. We were so flexible and enthusiastic. We just wanted to play for the love of the game."

Any patch of land was a potential cricketing location; wasteland, old recreation grounds and Savile Park. Najabat, who played many cameo knocks for the infant side, says "We were all young, free and single, and we were so inventive in the way we fixed up grounds and venues. There were no pre-bookings; we'd never heard of this. Usually, the neighbours didn't mind, just so long as we weren't up to mischief."

In the 1970s, there were no social or community centres for young Asians. They were left to their own devices, and often they had no seniors to turn to. So, they created their own entertainment and bonds of community. The QRM cricket team, and the QRM football side that emerged at the same time, were vital. Najabat comments, "In 2004 young Asians in Halifax have extended families and an infrastructure of youth groups and community centres to fall back on. In 1974 we had neither, and that's what makes the story of QRM even more significant, and remarkable."

Survival and Growth

Boston Hill: A New Era
Brian Heywood

The ground, in an ideal setting and surrounded by trees, is in marked contrast to the bleak exposed field at Old Laithe, which has the unenviable distinction of being one of the highest cricket grounds in Yorkshire.

Hebden Bridge Times and Gazette 1954

Drawing by Sue Brant

Ground improvements were essential to the survival of cricket clubs in the Calder Valley in the 1950s. Whilst other clubs disappeared, developments at Bridgeholme, Hebden Bridge, and Mytholmroyd Methodists enabled them to escape the collapsing Hebden Bridge League to the Halifax League. But the most ambitious venture was at Old Town.

Old Laithe had served Old Town well for over 50 years but in 1951 the committee realised that its inhospitable situation, 1000 feet above sea level, would be an increasing handicap as other clubs improved comfort levels for players and spectators. The match against Heptonstall Slack on 4 June 1955 was not the first at Old Laithe to be abandoned because of low cloud and fog.

By then Old Town were preparing their new and current ground on the Boston Hill estate at Wadsworth. The land belonged to the Heptonstall Rural District Council who had bought it from the Mitchell family for housing. After considerable delays in the granting of permits by the Ministry of Town and Country Planning, the club bought the land from the council for £450 in 1954. Grants of £300 from the National Playing Fields Association and £30 from the West Riding Playing Field Association contributed around 30% of the cost. The rest, plus all the labour, was provided by the club members who, among many other tasks, reassembled the Old Laithe pavilion at Boston Hill.

Old Town's first season at Boston Hill, 1957, was also the last of the Hebden Bridge League. Remaining loyal to this local league to the end, it was fitting that Old Town should win what proved to be the league's last match, the top four play-off final against Halifax Second XI at Thrum Hall. Old Town, dismissed for 75, bowled Halifax out for 55.

The loss of four teams from the Hebden Bridge League in the Autumn of 1957 threatened its future and that of its remaining clubs. The Old Town committee was prepared to arrange friendlies, but the cost of creating and maintaining Boston Hill made competitive cricket essential. They applied to join the Halifax and District Amateur Cricket Association. It was a wise step. The Hebden Bridge and District Cricket League, founded in 1894, had haemorrhaged clubs for the last time and was officially disbanded on 30 December 1957.

At Old Town's Annual General Meeting on 6 January 1958, President Raymond Ashworth revealed that the club had made firm their application. Five days later on 11 January, the First and Second teams of Old Town and Heptonstall Slack, the last remnants of the Hebden Bridge League, were admitted to the Halifax Association where they dominated the third division in 1958.

In 1959, along with SBCI, they were admitted to the second division of the Halifax League. The Boston Hill ground was crucial to Old Town's acceptance. The hard work of the members had paved the way for a new chapter in the club's history.

The committee's leadership of Old Town Cricket Club through the 1950's is impressive: the foresight to realise that a new, more hospitable ground would be necessary, the determination and skills to see the development through, the loyalty to stay with the Hebden Bridge League when they could have benefited by joining one of the Halifax leagues, and the wisdom to join the Association when the Hebden Bridge League was likely to fail. Raymond Ashworth was already looking to the challenges ahead:

> We have a lovely ground, but shall have to face heavy expenditure on up-to-date equipment if we are to keep it so. Another item required, and which I consider to be of paramount importance, is a good practice wicket. The present concrete pitches are far from satisfactory and can undermine the confidence of youngsters having to face up to fast bowling which rises far above the normal height.

(Old Town was formed in 1885, playing in the Hebden Bridge League from 1896)

The Opening of Station House 1952-1957
Brian Heywood

Players in the league will this season be testing Bridgeholme's new ground at Eastwood. It is understood that the wicket is in fine shape, but it will be some weeks before the outfield is up to the required standard.
Hebden Bridge Times and Gazette, 24 April 1953

Preparation of the Station House ground had been underway since the summer of 1952. Drainage, levelling and the laying of the square had been the priorities. The first match, against Hebden Bridge Salem in the first division of the Hebden Bridge and District League, was scheduled for 9 May 1953 but the ground was not quite ready and the game was switched to Salem Field. Bridgeholme captain John Martin hit 125 of his side's 222, the first century by a Bridgeholme batsman and the first time the team had scored 200.

The ground was opened ten days later on the evening of Tuesday 19

May, just a fortnight before the coronation of Queen Elizabeth II. The First XI beat Heptonstall Slack seconds by eight wickets in the Hebden Bridge League's 20 overs-a-side knockout cup, Jack Kaye taking 7 for 20 with his off-spinners as the visitors were dismissed for 40.

The first league match on the ground was played the following Saturday when the Second team beat Old Town seconds by 54 runs. The first eleven made their home league debut on 30 May and suffered one of only three defeats that season, replying to Birchcliffe's 174 with 99 all out.

With the square reasonably prepared, work continued apace on the outfield, including digging out the banking under the road to widen the playing area. In January 1954 an application to enter the Halifax Parish Cup was rejected, in part because the ground was deemed *unfit*, yet five months later Bridgeholme was selected to host the Hebden Bridge League's knockout final between Heptonstall Slack and Birchcliffe. Presenting the trophy, League President Dr AH Clegg congratulated the club "on the efforts they have made to make the field into a good ground."

Further improvements saw the club admitted to the Parish Cup and to the Halifax League for the 1956 season. "The advent of Bridgeholme was one of the year's successes," commented League Secretary NE Crossley at the League's AGM. "The club has shown a wonderful spirit in developing its ground, and has proved its intention of holding its own in the league."

There was further praise from the *Hebden Bridge Times* in April 1957:

> ... the biggest improvements have taken place on the Bridgeholme ground at Eastwood. For several weeks work has been going

on widening the field and painting the pavilion, and last weekend the overall picture of the ground gave a pleasing appearance.

Founded in 1951, Bridgeholme's progress on and off the field is a model for any new club. Within eight years, through careful planning, sustained effort and commitment, they were established in the top division of the Calder Valley's best amateur league and had created a ground to be proud of.

(Bridgeholme was formed in 1950)

A Scorebox from Nottingham: Part II
Rob Hardie

To the horror of everyone at Slaithwaite, the Nottingham scorebox, so generously given to them after the death of a former president, was to last only 40 years. In 1986 a fire swept through the structure, completely gutting the box and causing £20,000 of damage to the ground, practice kit, ground maintenance equipment and fertilisers.

A small temporary scoreboard was then erected until a permanent structure was unveiled at a ceremony on May 23 1987. The man who officially opened the building was club member Mr Harry Stones. A Slaithwaite loyalist since 1918, Stones was also at the unveiling of the original box in 1945. Unfortunately, a special match to mark the occasion between a *SC&BC* Select XI and a Holme Valley XI was called off due to rain.

Also at the clubhouse is a dedicated bench presented to Mr Stones. In 1988 the bench was given to him as the club's longest serving supporter and also holder of many roles at the club post 1918. As well as being a First XI player, Mr Stones occupied the positions of Second XI Captain, Secretary, Treasurer, groundsman and Vice-Chairman.

Home Sweet Home: Warrenside 1994-1997
Sam Christie

Few cricket clubs could match Bradley & Colnebridge Cricket Club's strength, character and determination. Spearheaded by Raymond Hawkyard, Bradley & Colnebridge withstood the ordeal of moving grounds and the refusal of Holliday Chemical Holdings to fund the move. They had initially agreed to provide £150,000.

Ironically, the club were asked to go to Warrenside in 1974 by Bradley Rangers Football Club when the proposed Clifton bypass threatened to run straight through the old Colnebridge ground, but they declined. Club Chairman and groundsman Raymond Hawkyard explains:

> We formed a committee with Bradley Rangers Football Club and we were both offered a move to Warrenside for £1,995. We couldn't afford to as we had no money but Bradley Rangers moved there. Fortunately the plans for the bypass fell through.

Twenty years later, Bradley & Colnebridge were dealt a double blow and, according to Hawkyard, they thought it was the day that the club was finally going to fold:

> On 4 February 1994, I received a letter from Holliday Chemical Holdings explaining they weren't going to give us any money towards finding a new ground, despite the fact they had agreed to fund the move with £150,000. The same day, the cricket club president came round to my house and told me that we had 30 days to get off the Colnebridge ground land.

Though planning permission to build on the Colnebridge ground was initially rejected because of objections from local residents, Hollidays were eventually given permission. Raymond Hawkyard recalls:

We wrote to the league, the mayor, councillors and local MPs, complaining at the way we had been treated. Hollidays offered us £20,000 but we ignored it and continued to write letters to the Sports Council. Eventually Hollidays improved their offer to £50,000. We thought we better accept this one because we believed it would be enough to fund the move.

The new Warrenside ground wasn't going to be complete until the beginning of the 1996 season, so where they were going to play their home matches for the remainder of the 1994 season and the whole of the following season? A relieved chairman comments:

We were extremely fortunate that in the Drakes League in 1994 and the Huddersfield Central League in 1995 there was an odd number of teams which allowed us to play at the ground that wasn't being used that week. If this wasn't the case, we certainly would have folded.

More setbacks were yet to follow when the ground was complete. According to club groundsman Hawkyard:

The pitch was diabolical and a bit dangerous during the 1996 season. It was far from ideal and we needed a new drainage system put in. We managed to get the money from Hollidays to fund the installation. The pitch needed flattening out as it sloped down to the square, then up again to the boundary. This cost £5,000 to complete.

In 1995 Club Treasurer, Alistair Sykes, successfully applied for £38,914 from the National Lottery to build a new pavilion. The work began in October 1996 and the pavilion was officially opened in July 1997 by local cricket VIP Alec Lodge. Current Acting Secretary and Treasurer David Moorhouse, along with his colleagues from Elite Systems, built the pavilion from scratch:

It took nine months to construct and the facilities in the new pavilion are far better than the old portakabin. Where we got changed before building the new pavilion was a temporary building but the new structure is a timber frame building, which is extremely solid and reliable.

Similar to many town or city centre sporting locations, there has also been trouble with local residents, most notably in 1996 when motorbikes were used to ruin the pitch and, most importantly, the square. A fence was erected, kindly paid for by Club President Mel Harrier. In addition, an orange mesh was set up to protect the square. Nevertheless, in 1997 a motorbike destroyed the fence and nearly prevented the club from playing scheduled matches. Hawkyard explains:

> I rang the league to say we could not play for a few weeks because a biker had done 16 spins on his bike and damaged the square. Fortunately I managed to repair the pitch the best I could and it was playable.

Despite all the damage done to the pitch, it is still in good condition mainly thanks to the efforts of Chairman and groundsman Raymond Hawkyard. He says, "It's not the worst in the league but it's not the best."

Bradley & Colnebridge League Representative and Sponsorship Secretary Steve Ashwell believes there has been a massive change in the Warrenside ground over the last decade. "It was originally just an area of spare land but the pavilion has been built with excellent facilities - considering we're an amateur cricket club. Both changing rooms have showers, and there is also an impressive tea room and scoreboard."

(Bradley and Colnebridge were established as Colnebridge in 1843. Their current incarnation began in 1959 and they play in the Huddersfield Central League)

Professionals

Neil Dansie
Brian Heywood

Neil Dansie is a former batsman for South Australia and was Todmorden's professional in 1955 and 56.

How did you come to the attention of the S. Australian selectors?

I had made a few runs in 'A' Grade and they had a look at me in the nets and then they selected me to play against New South Wales. That was in 1949. I went out to bat at 84 for 5 and made 36. I remember that Keith Miller was in the opposition and when I had got a few he walked past between overs and said to me "Keep going. You're batting well." That's hard to believe from an opponent these days, isn't it? That generosity of spirit started to disappear when all the money came into the game.

Which other Australian players did you meet at that time?

All of the 1948 team which toured England – Don Bradman, Arthur Morris, Ray Lindwall – all great players.

How did you come to hear of Todmorden's interest in you?

Arthur Richardson had played over here in the 1930s [for Bacup and Burnley]. I was approached through him.

What were your commitments during the week?

I would practise with the team and I coached everybody from the youngest to the oldest at the club. I ran nets for the juniors from 4pm till 8pm and one young man was always the first to arrive and the last to leave. I said at the time, with his determination and enthusiasm, he would go a long way in the game, and fifteen years later he was getting off the plane to play against Australia – Peter Lever.

What were your impressions of cricket in the Lancashire League?

Good. Every team had four or five exceptionally good cricketers. The grounds were mostly okay and the pitches were slow but quite good. I definitely returned home to Australia a much better player.

Which Todmorden players of that era do you recall?

All of them. I can tell you the whole team. There was Harold Dawson, John Crowther, John Ingham, Richard Crabtree, Kenny Walker, Peter Brownbridge, Colin Sunderland, Jack Hazeltine the wicketkeeper, Malcolm Heywood, Frank Saul, Ewart Clayton …

You did not return to Australia in the winter of 1955-56.

No. I spent that winter at Alf Gover's Cricket School in London. I went to be coached and to learn how to coach. One who was there nearly every day was Jim Laker. He bowled fabulous off-spinners and spent that winter perfecting his arm ball (one that didn't spin which he disguised so that it looked like his off-spinner) and of course the following summer he took his nineteen wickets against Australia at Old Trafford, the best ever performance by a bowler in a Test Match.

Who were your contemporaries towards the end of your career?

I played with the great West Indian Gary Sobers for South Australia. He could do everything, bat, bowl in every style, and field; the greatest all-rounder there has ever been. I remember Victoria's captain Bill Lawry saying how easily they were going to beat us. Les Favell, our captain, used this to motivate us. "Have you seen what Lawry has been saying about us?" Sobers replied quietly, "I think we might win this one, skipper," and then got a hundred, and five wickets. We won easily. Still, Lawry didn't give up and in his speech at the Victorian end-of-season dinner said they hadn't been beaten by South Australia, they'd been beaten by Sobers. Then a lady stood up and said, 'Excuse me Mr Lawry. If Victoria is so good how come eleven Victorians have been beaten by one West Indian?'

What made Don Bradman special?

His eye, allied to great footwork and balance. He was in position to play his shots faster than anyone I have ever seen. He just picked up the line and length of the ball so quickly. I batted with him in his very last innings in Grade cricket.

Who were the best pace bowlers you faced?

In Australia, Ray Lindwall and Keith Miller were obviously great bowlers. Wes Hall was a great bowler for the West Indies. The quickest was Frank Tyson in 1954. He *pro'd* for Todmorden after me, I believe. I once had to bat out the last over against Fred Trueman for South Australia. I survived the first seven balls and Trueman only ran in four paces for the last one. It was the quickest of the lot and bowled me. Great bowler!

Chris Balderstone (1940-2000)
Peter Redding

He began in Chesterfield with the County match between Leicestershire and Derbyshire, scored 51 not out by the close of play and rushed up the motorway to Doncaster to play against Brentford in the League Cup. He returned to Chesterfield the next day to complete his century. For many this would be a dream but for Chris Balderstone it was reality. Dual sporting careers are not uncommon, Denis Compton being the most famous example, but on 15th September 1975, Chris Balderstone made history, competing in two sporting events simultaneously.

He was a promising schoolboy at Paddock CC. He played for the senior side in the Huddersfield League before turning 15. In May 1958 he signed for hometown soccer club, Huddersfield, whose manager was the little known Bill Shankly. First team opportunities failed to come his way due to the presence of Denis Law and he had to wait almost a year for his debut, scoring against Cardiff City.

Like many in his era, he experienced the tough school that was Yorkshire County Cricket Club. He made his first-class debut in 1961 and went on to make just 68 appearances in 10 years, largely because he failed to register a first class century.

In 1965 he moved to Carlisle United for £7,000 and scored 68 goals in 369 games in one of the most successful spells of the club's history. He became a fan favourite at Brunton Park after scoring the penalty that briefly took the club to the top of the First Division in 1974/75. His time at Carlisle wasn't without its problems. In 1973 he was suspended and stripped of the captaincy after deciding to finish the County Cricket season rather than reporting for pre-season training.

He had to make a decision, and cricket made it for him. With Leicestershire since 1971, he was one of the most consistent batsmen in the country, and a key part of a successful Foxes side. In 1972 he was Man of the Match in the Benson and Hedges Cup Final, scoring 41 not out in a low scoring run chase, all the more sweet given that it was a win against Yorkshire.

In 1975, Leicestershire won their first County Championship title. Chris made 1,222 runs at 37 including 5 centuries, rewarded with a call up to the England Test side the following summer. The 1976 touring West Indian team was no side to make your debut against, however, and motivated by Tony Greig's infamous "we want to make them grovel" speech they went on to hammer England 3-0. He made two appearances in the series, the first at Headingley where he made 35 and 4 in a narrow West Indian win.

His second Test appearance was a memorable one, for Vivian Richards and Michael Holding who both produced career best performances. Chris found himself on the receiving end of both, first in the field when he spilled a chance to remove Richards on 151 off Derek Underwood, a moment he recalls well: "I don't think *Deadly* [Underwood] ever forgave me!" Richards went on to make 291. Chris then recorded a pair, bowled both times by Holding who picked up 14 wickets on the most docile of pitches.

Chris played 10 more years for Leicester after his two Test caps. He finished on 19,034 first class runs at an average of 34 including 32 centuries. His career best score, an unbeaten 181, came against Gloucestershire at Grace Road in 1984. He shares the second-wicket partnership record for Leicestershire, an unbroken 289 with David Gower against Essex at Grace Road in 1981.

Chris could also bowl. His left-arm spin claimed 310 first class wickets with career best figures of 6 for 25 against Hampshire at Southampton in 1978 and a hat-trick against Sussex at Eastbourne in 1976. Despite the Richards missed chance, he was a more than competent fielder, holding 210 first class catches.

Retiring in 1986 at the age of 45, Balderstone moved into umpiring, joining the First-Class umpires list in 1988. He would again get a brief taste of International cricket, standing in two One Day Internationals both featuring England and the touring South Africans of 1994 and 1998. He would surely have umpired in more International matches had it not been for his premature death in 2000 from cancer aged just 59.

Nirmal Nanan
Robert Hardie

Having tasted success with Dilip Doshi and Madan Lal, Meltham looked overseas once more, to the Caribbean instead of east into Asia. Nirmal Nanan, born on the 19th of August 1951 in Preysel, Trinidad, signed in time for the 1977 cricket season.

Nanan was a fine batsman, learned under the tutelage of the magnificent Garfield Sobers. His record of three consecutive batting awards during his three years of Huddersfield League cricket with Meltham still exists. In addition, Nanan's impressive batting displays helped Meltham's first XI to the Byrom Shield in 1978.

Nanan left the club after his record busting 1979 campaign to continue his county championship career at Nottinghamshire. He played 35 matches, scoring 925 runs at an average of 15.67, with three half centuries.

Perhaps an inability to hit the big scores at the highest level kept Nanan from being called up for the West Indies. But the likes of Colin Croft, Joel Garner, Larry Gomes, Gordon Greenidge, Desmond Haynes, Michael Holding, Roy Fredericks, Alvin Kallicharran, Malcolm Marshall, Andy Roberts and the legendary Viv Richards made it something of an impossible task.

As well as Nottinghamshire County Cricket Club, Nanan played top flight cricket for provincial sides South Trinidad and Central Trinidad before and after his time in England. His first class career lasted from the age of 18 in 1969 up until his retirement aged 33 in 1984.

Gary Sobers
John Garnham

Sir Garfield Sobers was one of the great all-rounders of international cricket. What many people will not know is that he was a Paddock professional in the early 1960s, when he hit 62 in a Huddersfield League fixture against Golcar. Later he said, "In a way, playing league cricket makes me try harder than in a Test."

He was named Wisden Cricketer of the Year in 1964, selected as one of the five cricketers of the century in 2000 and knighted for his services to cricket in 1975.

He captained the West Indies in 39 Tests, winning 9 and losing 10. He gained 93 caps and made 7,999 runs in a Test career spanning 20 years. He started and finished his Test career against England: 1954 at Kingston and 1974 at Port of Spain.

Sobers signed for Nottinghamshire from Barbados and ended his first-class career for South Australia. He scored 28,314 first-class career runs and took 1,043 wickets with his best haul 9 for 49.

Rahul Mankad
Michael Ward

Rahul Mankad was a talented cricketer, yet some cricket fans might think of his father, Vinoo, or brother Ashok, when they hear the name Mankad. One place that would never happen is Cleckheaton.

22 year old Rahul became Cleckheaton's first ever overseas player in 1977 and stayed at Moorend for four years, scoring over 3,000 runs.

In his debut season, Cleckheaton's second in the Bradford League, he was the club's top run scorer with 774. He also persuaded other Indian Test cricketers to play. Yvindra Singh, *Sunny*, was another, albeit shorter, success, taking 17 wickets in just 4 games, followed by Indian Test bowler Suru Nayak and in 1980, Vijay Mohan Raj.

In 1978, Mankad achieved an aggregate of 1251 runs, a league record that stood for 15 years. Cleckheaton, however, finished second bottom and had to re-apply for membership of the Bradford League. He helped make history in 1979 when Cleckheaton gained promotion to the Bradford League's first division for the very first time.

Rahul never played a Test or ODI for India. He played first class cricket for his hometown, Mumbai. In 47 matches he scored 2111 runs and in limited spells of bowling, took 7 wickets for 250. Mumbai won the prestigious Ranji Trophy 7 times during his time with the club.

Ghulam Parkar
Aaron Gales

On October 25th 1955 in Maharashtra, India, Ghulam Parkar was born. He was an extremely talented cricketer who represented his country in both forms of international game.

He played only one Test, unfortunate to come along at a time when Indian selectors demanded instant success, and after failing in his first game, he was never picked again.

However, despite this blip on his CV, he had a truly phenomenal first-class career which saw a brief interlude at Mirfield.

A dashing opening batsman with a wonderful array of attacking shots and an extremely athletic fielder, he was a natural for the one-day form of the game. He played ten times for his country and was an integral part of the Bombay side. In the Ranji Trophy he scored over 3,000 runs at an average of just under 50. He formed an explosive partnership with the great Sunil Gavaskar, once scoring 421 runs in one match. In all first class matches he scored more than 4,000 runs at an average of over 42, playing a total of 68 matches.

Clive Lloyd
Aaron Gales

Clive Lloyd was truly one of the greatest players ever to play the game. A batsman who quite simply dominated bowling attacks and scored over 7,000 Test runs at an average of over 46. Few people know that he once turned out for Holmfirth.

He was also one of the most successful captains. Under him, from 1974 to 1985, the West Indies became the dominant Test team, destroying all comers and at one stage going 27 matches undefeated, including an unprecedented run of 11 successive victories. They also won two World Cups: in 1975 (when Lloyd scored a majestic century in the Final) and 1979. Lloyd also led them to the Final in 1983 when they were surprisingly beaten by India. He is the first West Indian player to make 100 appearances for the Test side.

He was named a Wisden Cricketer of the Year in 1971.

Since retiring from the game, Lloyd has remained heavily involved in cricket and was an ICC match referee from 2001 to 2006 and is currently managing the West Indian cricket team.

Young Gun Turned Pro! Paul Jarvis
Michael Ward

Paul Jarvis already had a claim to fame when he arrived at Mount Pleasant to begin a year with Batley Cricket club in 1983. Two years earlier he had become Yorkshire's youngest player at just sixteen years old. The right-arm fast bowler from Redcar was widely predicted to have a great future in the game.

The move to Batley was mutually beneficial for both parties as Jarvis gained much needed experience which, in turn, enabled him to take the wickets that helped Batley recover from relegation the previous year. Fresh from this positive spell he returned to Yorkshire, only to spend the next two years nursing various injuries. Some believe these injuries were the result of over bowling in his teens and they would constantly blight his career.

Undeterred, Jarvis marked his return to fitness with his first county cap. In 1987 he helped Yorkshire to win the Benson and Hedges Cup, taking 4 wickets for 43 runs in the Final versus Northants. Jarvis also took a career high number of 81 wickets.

This form led to his first England call-up for the winter tour of Pakistan, New Zealand and Australia. He took 4 wickets at Christchurch against New Zealand. However, he only took 2 wickets in the following game, which led to him being dropped for the last Test. He was recalled for the home series against the West Indies, scoring 29 not out and taking 4 for 107 at Lord's. Unfortunately, a back strain caused him not just to miss the rest of the series, but a whole year of Test cricket.

Jarvis fought his way back against Australia at Lord's but failed to take a wicket. He repeated this at Edgbaston and was dropped. He then took part in an England rebel tour of the then Apartheid South Africa. This resulted in most players, including Jarvis, being banned from Test cricket for three years.

Following the early removal of the ban, Jarvis was picked for England's tour of India and Sri Lanka. In the first two Tests he took 4 wickets as India thrashed England twice. Despite having done enough, he was dropped. Jarvis' last ever Test came in Colombo against Sri Lanka. He will remember the tour for his Man-of-the-Match performance in a One Day International against India.

Jarvis joined Sussexfor the beginning of the 1993 season. He made a bright start with 51 wickets, earning him his second county cap. Unfortunately, he spent most of the next three seasons on the sidelines with injuries. He left for Somerset in 1998, yet fared little better there and ended his career in county cricket in 2000. Despite appearing to have the world at his feet, bad luck with injuries cost Paul Jarvis the chance to show the full extent of his talent. He played 9 Tests and 16 ODIs for England and took over 650 First Class wickets.

Ronnie Hart
Ashley Ball

The right-handed Kiwi made an impression with bat as well as behind the stumps and was also known to have a bowl, yet he only represented his native country on one occasion in a One Day International.

Ronald Terence Hart was born in Lower Hutt, Wellington, in 1961. In New Zealand he played for both his hometown sides, Wellington and Central Districts.

In his one appearance for New Zealand he scored a disappointing 3 runs against the West Indies at St. John's, Antigua, in 1985. He was never to be called up again.

Hart managed well over 2,500 first-class runs from just 51 matches; this left him with a respectable batting average of 29.51. Hart was very much an emergency bowler and he failed to claim a wicket in first class games; however, he did gain one dismissal in a List A game. His bowling style was off-break.

His time in local cricket came at Gomersal.

Top Amateur

Dropping Anchor for the Team
Ian Hodgson

Name: Stephen Rushworth, Broad Oak
Position: Ex-captain/batting all-rounder
Length of captaincy?

I've been captain of the first team for four years, although that hasn't been consecutive years.

Other clubs you've played for?

I played for Leymoor for most of my junior career although I did go for one year up at Golcar because Leymoor didn't have an U13 team. Then when I was 17 I went to play for Broad Oak as I was told that I could play at a higher level.

Strengths as a batsmen?

I've altered my game a bit ... we've got quite a few aggressive young players so I tend to occupy the crease a bit more, so we don't lose too many wickets at one end, and let the young lads play some shots at the other ... I get a bit of stick for being a bit negative and boring but I've put myself down the order because we've got some good young players and I want to give them a go.

Strengths as a bowler?

The wickets at Broad Oak are pretty good, so it can be quite difficult ... Dropping down to Section 'B', you can get away with bowling the odd bad ball but in Section 'A' you get punished. If the wickets are doing a bit and it's quite wet then it obviously helps me more and I may be able to get it to swing a bit as well.

High points?

In 1985, my debut season, we played Honley and were bowled out for 31. They won by 110 runs, and I batted for close to 20 overs and scored about three. We then played in the Final of the Sykes Cup and my best friend Simon Hoyle and myself opened the batting; we were both 17 when the Final started. The Final got rained off that many times, though, I was 18 by the time we won it! Also that year, the juniors won the Walker Cup; Simon Hoyle and myself knocked off 140 runs without losing any wickets against Lascelles Hall. The second team won the Paddock Shield so for all three teams to win something was a great achievement.

Low points?

Would have to be getting relegated from Section 'A' ... we had three or four players who were related to each other and when one of them left, all the others left as well, so it was a case of rebuilding. Then we got a bloke who joined and his dad put a lot of money into the club so we could bring in a professional ... Last season the professional went home halfway through; he wasn't making as many runs as he should have ... We missed his 10 good overs in each game.

First century?

Was against Skelmanthorpe when I got 121, batting with Jonny Greaves and he was the youngest ever person to get a hundred at the time. We had a partnership of about 220 runs.

Most memorable match?

Would be the Semi-Final in 1985. We only scored 150, which at Broad Oak isn't really a match-winning score. We got them 30 for 4 and then all out for 80, so there was a big celebration after. The final was obviously good to win but the gloss was taken off slightly because it was called off due to rain so many times. We were playing a team much stronger than us, so on paper the Semi-Final was like Barnsley beating Chelsea!

Hanging Heaton Collection

Abdul Qadir
Craig Bamford

Born in 1955 in Lahore, Abdul Qadir Khan made his first-class debut during 1975 playing in local Pakistan competitions. His role was as a leg-spin bowler and his personalised run-up and appealing style made him a favourite. He had a variety of deliveries and was one of the most successful spin bowlers at a time when spin bowling was rare. Qadir gave other spin bowlers the belief to achieve and he is one of the many memorable players to walk onto the field at Hanging Heaton.

He made his Test debut on home soil against England in 1977. During his second Test series here in England in 1978, he was injured. He didn't make a real impact until 1982, when he helped Pakistan to a memorable victory against the English. During that season Qadir was the first Pakistani to take 100 wickets.

In 1987, he took ten wickets in the series win in England. The same season saw him achieve new heights as he became the first Pakistani bowler to reach the 200 wicket milestone, including a record best of 9 for 56 and 4 for 45.

The great Pakistani cricketer spent 20 years playing First-Class cricket, reaching 960 career wickets.

Dilip Vengsarkar
Aaron Gales

Over a period of 15 years, Dilip Vengsarkar batted for India in over 100 Tests and One Day Internationals, totting up over 10,000 runs. Little do many people know that he also once played for Hanging Heaton in the Bradford League, at a time when he was rated the top Test batsman in the world.

He made his debut against New Zealand in Auckland in 1975, a match which India won. He made two low scores and was out of the side for a short while. On his recall he scored 8 centuries in 16 Test matches and was named Wisden Cricketer of the Year in 1987.

He scored six centuries against the great West Indian bowling attack, sharing in a record unbroken second wicket stand of 344 with Sunil Gavaskar. He also became the first Test batsman to score three consecutive centuries at Lord's, a record that has yet to be matched. He retired in 1992, second only to Gavaskar for runs and centuries scored. He is the current chairman of the Indian selectors.

Angela Hepworth - Helping Out
Zak Data

You could argue that the tea lady is an unsung heroine. According to Angela Hepworth of Hanging Heaton, the job is a whole lot more than just making the tea. "I'm heavily involved with helping out at the club." she states, "and all of the other helpers put in work behind the scenes. We all help with various tasks which need to be completed in order to keep the housekeeping up to scratch. It's not just doing teas, although that is our main priority."

Angela's day starts at 7am when she heads off to the local supermarket to buy ingredients and snacks. She offers a wide range of filled sandwiches, including chicken, tuna and the spectators' favourite, cheese and onion. She makes sure there's plenty.

She was initially drawn into the club because of her husband, Tony. The club then asked "Will you help us out by doing teas?" Angela couldn't refuse.

Drawing by Sue Brant

Angela has the club's interests at heart. Just walking around the club you can feel the wholesome family atmosphere that keeps the club together. "We're very proud of Hanging Heaton Cricket Club."

Iqbal Qasim
Craig Bamford

Mohammad Iqbal Qasim was born in 1953 in Karachi. He played in 50 Test matches for Pakistan and 15 One Day Internationals. In the early 1980s he played some of his cricket at Hanging Heaton.

The slow left-armer finished his Test career with 171 wickets, with 3.5 wickets a match and an economy rate of 2.21.

Qasim was a slow bowler but in actual fact, he delivered the ball at a much faster pace than most, and didn't necessarily rely on great turn, often deceiving batsmen with variations.

He is remembered by most for his performance during the tense clash between India and Pakistan in the 1987 Test series, when he took 9 for 121, dismissing Sunil Gavaskar for 96 and helping his country to their first series win on Indian soil.

Among Pakistani slow bowlers only Abdul Qadir had taken more Test wickets. He could not be relied upon with the bat and the pictures of him taking a blow from Bob Willis against England in the First Test at Edgbaston in 1978 underline this fact.

V.V.S. Laxman
Craig Bamford

Vangipurappu Venkata Sai is how we spell it, but for pronouncing it, I think we'll stick to VVS. Many of us also don't know that Laxman once played cricket at Hanging Heaton, in the Bradford League.

He made his Test debut against South Africa in 1996. Despite be-ing more comfortable in the middle order he was asked to open. After three years with no real success, he scored a huge 167 against the Aussies. He then made his point to the selectors, saying that he wasn't happy opening the innings, and was subsequently dropped for almost a year.

On his return in 2001 against the Australians, Laxman leaped over Sunil Gavaskar's record with 236 not out. He hit three ODI and two Test centuries during the 2003 tour of Australia.

After touring England last year, he joined Lancashire in the English County Championship, where he replaced Brad Hodge. In five games he scored 380 runs at an average of 54.28, including two tons and two half-centuries. With India the same year, he scored his twelfth Test hundred against the Australians.

Currently, VVS Laxman is captaining the Deccan Chargers in the Indian Cricket League.

The Great Pavilion of Hanging Heaton
Mark Whitcombe

It stands there grand, towering, omniscient. The centre of social life. Come Summer, Autumn, Winter or Spring it is there, proud symbol for a proud club.

As you enter you can smell the ale, smell the history. Photographs remembering the glory years. And amid the televisions, the pool tables, the slot machines, we find the trophy cabinet. The scorers do their job watching from the bottom window, taking note. Benches are placed accordingly. Cars park close by. And at the top we have the balcony, overlooking the wicket, it watches.

An inspiration. Heroes die and the memory of matches fade, but the pavilion stands on. It does not shake to wind or bow to the four seasons.

History Man, Ismail Dawood
Zak Data

Ismail Dawood is a popular figure among cricket fans in Yorkshire. He was the first Yorkshire-born Asian to play first-class cricket for the White Rose County.

Dawood was born in Dewsbury, Yorkshire, starting as a junior at Hanging Heaton. He played for England U19s against India in 1994, West Indies in 1994-95 and South Africa in 1995. While with Glamorgan, Dawood showed that he was a useful lower-order batsman. He scored 102 against Gloucestershire at Cardiff after being promoted to open the batting following injuries to other players. Later in the season, he created a new county record by not conceding a bye as Lancashire totalled 556 for 6 declared at Blackpool. Dawood left Glamorgan at the end of the 1999 season. After a spell out of cricket, he returned to Yorkshire in 2003. In 2004, the disappointing form of the Yorkshire wicketkeeper became an opportunity for Dawood to step in. After impressing in the Second XI, he made his first-team debut in the Twenty

20 Cup match against Derbyshire. He is now back at Hanging Heaton and enjoying cricket once again.

Aside from cricket, Ismail enjoys nothing better than to take his younger cousins to Tropical World in Roundhay Park and have lunch with his mum. He is also a big fan of stand-up comedy and spends a lot of his free time attending comedy clubs in the area. He also enjoys reading, horse racing, travelling to new places and learning about new cultures, customs and Egyptology.

(Hanging Heaton play in the Bradford League. The club began in 1876)

Memorable Matches

Halifax Parish Cup Final, King Cross v Triangle
Sat 25 July – Mon 3 August 1953
Brian Heywood

The Parish Cup Final of 1953 remains one of the best, and most protracted, in a history which dates to 1888.

King Cross was the most powerful team in the district at the time.

The First XI were riding high in the Yorkshire League and the second team, top of the Halifax League's first division, were favourites to secure the Parish Cup against midtable Triangle.

Only 40 minutes play was possible on Saturday 25 July. Handicapped by a wet ball, Triangle did well to remove both openers and restrict King Cross to 43 for 2.

With no play possible two evenings later, the match was postponed until the following Saturday when a crowd of over 1000 saw 390 runs scored and 10 wickets fall. A solid 53 from D Priestley was the cornerstone of King Cross's 151 for 4 before the compulsory suspension of the innings. Triangle recovered from 24 for 2, thanks to a third wicket stand of 119 between F Wolfenden (69) and B Hunter (66) and had reached 151 for 3 when King Cross elected to resume batting. A rapid 58 from JD Uttley steered the favourites to 282 for 9 when bad light ended play at 9pm.

Six more runs were added on Monday evening before A Booth (4 for 68) ended the King Cross innings at 288.

It appeared to be enough when overnight batsmen Wolfenden and Widdop were dismissed at 175 for 5, but the left-handed E Ingham, a former King Cross player, farmed the bowling and struck 13 boundaries in a magnificent 75 to keep Triangle in the game.

The result was still in the balance when the persevering Uttley, who followed his 58 with 6 wickets for 73, had Ingham stumped at 271 for 8, but another former King Cross man, Donald Garside, kept his nerve to hit the winning runs.

Triangle won by one wicket. The Cup was presented by a former president of the King Cross club, the Mayor of Halifax, Councillor Harold Pickles JP.

(The Halifax Parish Challenge Cricket Cup was initiated in 1897, open to any cricket club playing within Halifax Parish. King Cross began in 1878 as King Cross Wesleyans. Triangle were founded in 1862. Both play in the Halifax League)

20th Century (2)

Booth v Booths
Brian Heywood

In 1957 Booth Cricket Club hosted a most unusual cricket match on behalf of Johnny Wardle's benefit fund.

On Sunday 28 July Booth played a team of Booths! Captained by Yorkshire spin bowler Arthur Booth, the visiting team was:

H Booth (Elland)
W Booth (Marsden)
J Booth (Werneth)
D Booth (Bankfoot)
G Booth (Kirkburton)
G Booth (Yorkshire Colts)
B Booth (Lancashire)
D Booth (Featherstone)
Arthur Booth (Lancashire)
Arthur Booth (Littleborough)
Arthur Booth (Yorkshire)

(Booth Cricket Club, near Hebden Bridge, was established in 1893 and plays in the Halifax League)

Bridgeholme v Luddendenfoot St. Mary's
Saturday 8 May 1954, Station House, Eastwood
Brian Heywood

Luddendenfoot St Mary's had made a good start to their 1954 season in the Hebden Bridge & District League but faced a stiff test in their fourth match away to Bridgeholme, the reigning champions.

Bridgeholme's 107 all out looked more than enough as Luddendenfoot collapsed to 24 for 6. Then followed an astonishing blitz by J Helliwell, who smashed his way to 80 not out. No one else made double figures as the visitors won without further loss.

Luddendenfoot

Drawing by Sue Brant

Bridgeholme 107 all out: W Davies 46, M Smith 6-22

Luddendenfoot St Mary's

H Fisher	b Whittaker		4
D Bale	c Albinson	b Whittaker	3
J Fernyhough	b Whittaker		4
D Ashley	c W Davies	b Whittaker	0
L Jackson	c Whittaker	b A Martin	9
A Gawn	b Albinson		2
J Helliwell	not out		80
W Warburton	not out		7
Extras			3
Total (for 6 wickets) 112			

Luddendenfoot St Mary's won by 4 wickets. The victory sent Luddendenfoot clear at the top of the table, a position they held for the rest of the season. They won 14 and drew 3 of their twenty matches, totalling 33 points, six clear of their nearest rivals.

(Luddendenfoot was established in 1862, playing in the Halifax League)

1962 Heavy Woollen Cup Final
Mirfield v Hanging Heaton
James Norbury

The cricket season of 1962 will forever be remembered by all associated with Mirfield CC. That summer saw Mirfield lift the Heavy Woollen Cup for the first time, during a purple patch when Mirfield claimed the Central Yorkshire League title from 1958 to 1960.

Despite Mirfield's league dominance, they entered the 1962 Heavy Woollen Cup Final as underdogs against the highly fancied Hanging Heaton. Heaton were going well in the league and would eventually go on to capture the title. Following an epic clash at Savile Town, it was Mirfield who emerged victorious.

The victory was nothing more than Mirfield deserved after a gritty and hard fought performance against tough opposition. It was a match in which no one player particularly stood out from the others, but instead pulled together to produce an inspired display on both batting and fielding fronts.

The *Mirfield twins*, Colin Peacock and Clive Brook, opened the batting but the legendary pairing were unable to get going as Brook was caught for one. It was a huge shock for the Mirfield XI, as the pair had been one of the major factors in the club's success over the previous seasons.

While many teams may have collapsed after losing such an important player so early on in a cup final, Mirfield stood firm. They lost Grace to a catch by Smith, and were 4 for 2, but they soon managed to improve after this, however, and a successful stand developed between Peacock and Rigg.

Savile Town - undated

Despite a couple of anxious moments for the pair, including a missed catch behind the wicket and a shout for lbw against Peacock, they were able to notch up 64 between them before Peacock succumbed to an lbw appeal on 46. Rigg was eventually bowled for 23, leaving Mirfield 76 for 4. Ellis and Hodgson continued to frustrate the Hanging Heaton attack, and Mirfield finished their innings on a respectable 110 for 5.

Hanging Heaton must have fancied their chances, especially considering the form they had shown in the cup and league throughout the season. They were, however, overcome by a stubborn Mirfield bowling attack that was quick to take advantage of some sloppy batting from the league leaders. Clive Brook was quick to make amends for his poor batting performance with an impressive bowling effort. He bowled five maidens in 17 overs and took 4 wickets at a cost of 35 runs. Bert Wilcock was equally influential, taking 4 wickets for just 23 runs.

A local newspaper wrote:

Many spectators in attendance at Savile Town predicted the Final would run into a second day. This was not the case, however, as Hanging Heaton were all out for 81 to complete a convincing and famous victory for Mirfield. The trophy was presented by the Mayor of Dewsbury to proud captain Clive Brook who was delighted that Mirfield had won the prestigious trophy for the first time in their history.

Ramadhin, Sobers and Gilchrist
Peter Davies

In 1963 Sonny Ramadhin was in devastating form. In four matches for Golcar he took 27 wickets for 92 runs and he and Chester Watson bowled Golcar to the Sykes Cup Final. In the first round Ramadhin took 5 for 27 as Almondbury were bowled out for 68. In the second round Watson demolished Primrose Hill with 7 for 46. Golcar looked doomed in the Semi-Final, defending a meagre 92 all out, but Ramadhin's 9 for 19 skittled Holmfirth for 54. Unfortunately, neither Ramadhin nor Watson was available for the Final which Paddock won by 7 wickets.

Golcar's league match against Paddock on 19 May 1964 featured probably the most enticing professional confrontation the Huddersfield & District League had ever seen. The Paddock professional was cricket's greatest all-rounder, Gary Sobers, while Golcar had hired the scourge of league batsmen, Roy Gilchrist, for the day. Honours between the West Indian pros ended even. Sobers hit 62 of Paddock's 150 all out, while Gilchrist took 7 for 59.

Mytholmroyd v Barkisland
Parish Cup Second Round 1998
Russell Eggar

1998 was a year that did not promise much for Mytholmroyd Cricket Club. Struggling with their league form and failing to attract new players, the club was in a period of transition. With a bid in the pipeline to win a lottery grant to improve facilities at Ewood Holmes, they were at a point where the cricket took a back seat to the administrative work needed to improve the general condition and status of the club. Club captain at the time Martyn Astin remarked "The club was at a fairly low ebb."

The season produced one of the club's most memorable matches. One that is still re-lived in the public houses of Mytholmroyd.

The coveted Parish Cup was a welcome distraction from the First XI's inconsistent league form, but a second-round draw against runaway league leaders Barkisland was a different challenge altogether. As the overwhelming underdogs, the team knew that they had nothing to lose.

It started on a Sunday afternoon at Mytholmroyd. When rain delayed the start of play in the morning, it looked as if the game would continue through the week. As the game progressed the intensity of this *David v Goliath* encounter increased. Jon Russell remembers the feeling well "There was a lot of pressure even though we weren't expected to win the game."

Mytholmroyd finished their innings with a score of 141 for 9 with Astin scoring an impressive 80. They had dealt well with the pressure. Barkisland started their reply on the Sunday night, managing to see out

20 overs while confidently scoring 60 for 1.

Barkisland returned to Ewood Holmes a couple of days later to finish the job. Tuesday brought with it a dry track and outfield and limited hopes of Mytholmroyd progress. None of the players or spectators could have imagined how the final few overs were going to unfold. Astin didn't expect it to go any other way than a Barkisland win: "We were coming back to get finished off."

Mytholmroyd   **Drawing by Sue Brant**

Barkisland reached 131 for 6 and it looked like the match was all but over. A couple of big hits would settle it. Seven overs left and still a faint hope for Mytholmroyd. They were trying to keep the opposition out there for as long as possible. A couple of maidens bowled and the mighty Barkisland looked nervous. The tension from Sunday returned. The game came down to the final two overs with Russell bowling from the top end with his medium-pace, accurate trundlers and Jon Bamford at the bottom end bowling medium-pace away swingers. All of a sudden the bowling attack was questioning the bottle and the nerve of the Barkisland batsmen. They now needed just six runs to win, but Royd could feel them crumbling.

Russell's last over, a couple of singles and a wicket. Bamford's last over, three runs to score and three wickets left. The first ball swung and the already nervous batman took a large swing and missed. With the second ball, Bamford had the batter caught behind.

139 for 8. Four balls left and two wickets remaining

The next man in to bat was the experienced Brian Crabtree and as soon as he stepped up it was clear he was trying to do what the others before him should have done and hit the ball out the ground. With a little dance down the track and a big swing he missed the ball and was stumped by wicketkeeper Astin.

139 for 9. Three balls left and one wicket remaining.

The tension was unbearable. The last man came out and connected so firmly with the first ball that it was a certain four.

Game over, or so they thought. But a miraculous dive at deep mid-wicket prevented the boundary.

Two balls left, still one wicket needed, three runs to win.

With their hearts in their mouths, the crowd watched on as once again the last man connected with the ball but could only scramble a single.

140 for 9. One ball left, two runs needed for Barkisland to go into the next round and a single needed to force a replay.

A game that had taken two days to play out had come down to one solitary ball. Astin recalls "The batter got a little inside edge; a nightmare for any wicketkeeper and it went past my gloves, hit my leg and trickled away about 10 feet. A deafening 'YES' from the batsmen saw them running for the single. I ran for the ball, grabbed it and in one swift motion, turned, ran and with an underarm lob threw the ball at the stumps."

The ground erupted in ecstasy as the bails fell to the floor before the batsman could ground his bat. Mytholmroyd had produced an amazing win over the impressive Barkisland line-up by one run.

(Mytholmroyd was founded in the 1890s, Barkisland in 1899. They play in the Halifax and Huddersfield Leagues respectively)

Achievement

1963: Mirfield's Double
James Norbury

1963 was the season when Mirfield enjoyed a level of success rarely seen before, or indeed after, in the Central Yorkshire Cricket League.

With just one victory in their opening six league matches, the league title was beginning to look highly unlikely. Then big performances against Heckmondwike and Chickenley lifted them to fourth in the table, within five points of leaders Batley.

The next two league games were both played against Wakefield. Barry Wood scored an unbeaten 54, continuing impressive form that would take him into first-class cricket the following season. He played for Lancashire, Derbyshire and England, in 12 Tests and 13 one day internationals, scoring 768 runs in the process.

Mirfield were also turning heads in the Heavy Woollen Cup. After a comprehensive win over Dewsbury in the third round, they hung on against Ossett to secure a place in the Final.

Following league wins over Cleckheaton and Hanging Heaton, people began dreaming of the *double*. The first stage came on 9 August when Mirfield and Batley met in the Heavy Woollen Cup Final. Mirfield went into the game as the form team as Batley had endured a recent dismal run in the league. While Mirfield were favourites to retain the prestigious cup, few could have predicted the ease with which they would do so. Batley were on the end of a humiliating thrashing as they were all out in just over half an hour, accumulating just 33 runs. *The Dewsbury Reporter* referred to the innings as "thirty-eight minutes of furious fast bowling." The fast bowlers in question were Mellor and Peacock. Mellor took a staggering 7 wickets for just 15 runs, while Peacock took 3 for 10. Both managed to do this in 10 overs each. Peacock scored 21 not out to complete the nine-wicket demolition of one of Mirfield's closest title rivals. The awards were presented to the proud players by Mr RA Sheard, President of Heckmondwike CC and the Dewsbury & District Cricket League.

The Reporter called it a "photo-finish league championship" involving Mirfield and surprise contenders Dewsbury. Mirfield entertained Heckmondwike in their second-to-last game of the season and just about managed to hang on for a draw. Dewsbury were, however, defeated by Ossett, which meant that the title would go to Mirfield if rain washed out the matches the following weekend.

In the end, the final week's fixture went ahead and Mirfield were presented with a tricky visit to Hanging Heaton. Mirfield built a total of 142 with the help of Wood who scored 74 not out. Hanging Heaton made it to 96 for 3 before rain brought the game to a close and, in doing so, signalled the completion of a memorable league and cup *double* by Mirfield.

Club legend Clive Brook would later go on to say that captaining the side in 1963 was his greatest ever achievement in cricket. Colin Peacock won the league batting award. The Mirfield team that scooped the *double* contained key individuals such as Brook, Peacock, Barry Wood, Bert Wilcock and Allan Mellor, who all put in consistent, match-winning performances. However, when these players were not firing on all cylinders, there were always players in the squad who could make the step up. The league season was a long slog and it was a major team effort that enabled Mirfield to take the championship at the end of the campaign.

Mirfield did not win the league title again until 1990 when they matched the success of 1963 by also winning the Heavy Woollen Cup in the same season.

Handy Andy Spencer
Zak Data

Andy Spencer has been the groundsman at Scholes Cricket Club for 15 years and has never regretted this one moment. The remarkable thing about Andy is that he manages to balance his full-time job as a driver, while at the same maintaining the ground in a perfect condition.

Andy is employed full-time driving a mini-bus which transports disabled people, young and old, to and from a day centre. So how does he fit in his duties for Scholes? Luckily, Andy receives a four-hour break during which he manages to drive to New Popplewell Lane and make sure the square is prepared for the next match.

Andy took an interest in groundsmanship through a friend, and previous groundsman John Ratcliffe showed him the ropes. The

ECB and Institute of Groundsmen run day courses. "These courses are all very well and it is great that the craft is being recognised professionally; however, there is nothing better than hands-on experience. I learnt a massive amount by watching various video tapes and talking to professional groundsmen," he states.

Andy was proud when Scholes were the recipients of the Central Yorkshire League "Best Kept Ground" award in 2004. He recalls how the umpires graded the grounds, 'We had a decent summer that year. I didn't expect to win the award. I just do what I do to the best of my ability and hope people take note.'

Andy confessed that one day he wouldn't mind taking on a young apprentice. "I think to make it as a successful groundsman you've got to be hardworking and committed. You have got to enjoy your own company and be enthusiastic. Aim to be the best you can, enjoy your craft and you will be rightfully rewarded."

Rex Holt, The Perfect Ten!
Jon O'Shea

It's unavoidable that some days nothing will go your way, no matter how hard you try. On other days though, you just can't put a foot wrong. Former Northowram Hedge Top bowler Rex Holt made the short trip to Stainland's Memorial Ground on the 13 May 1979 and achieved every bowler's dream, the perfect ten.

Stainland CRICKET CLUB V Northowram C. CLUB — Innings of Stainland, played at Stainland on 13th May 1979

BATSMEN	RUNS SCORED	HOW OUT	BOWLER	TOTAL
hoswld	42	Bowled	R.Holt	6
ellwthwaite	4,4,4,1,1,2,2,1,2,1,2,1	Bowled	R.Holt	24
owa	1,1,1,4	L.B.W	R.Holt	7
melygge	1,1	Bowled	R.Holt	3
chase	2,1	Bowled	R.Holt	3
icholson		Bowled	R.Holt	0
thwell		NOT OUT		0
thwaite		ct c.Howl	R.Holt	0
hoswld		Bowled	R.Holt	0
urphy		L.Spencer	R.Holt	0
cclygge		Nfcrthug	R.Holt	0

TOTAL AT THE FALL OF EACH WICKET AND NO. OF OUTGOING BATSMAN

1 FOR	2 FOR	3 FOR	4 FOR	5 FOR	6 FOR	7 FOR	8 FOR	9 FOR	10 FOR	11
37	39	46	46	47	47	47	47	47		
3	2	5	6	8	8	9	10	11		

BYES — LEG BYES 1 — WIDES — NO BALLS — EXTRAS 4 — TOTAL 47 FOR 10 WKTS

"Four foot nine tall and nearly four foot wide!" according to former Hedge Top wicketkeeper Graham Spencer. Rex was a Second XI regular, versatile medium-quick bowler and pin-sharp fieldsman at mid-off. He was capable of swinging the ball both ways, making batsmen strain to pick his line, forcing mistakes and picking up regular *five-fors*. Graham Spencer's dad, Ian, who kept wicket on that memorable day at the Memorial Ground, believes Rex to be the most accomplished Second XI player he saw perform in the Halifax League.

By the time Stainland's sorry innings came to a close at 47 all out, Rex had the near-flawless figures of 10 wickets for 15 runs from 16 overs (including 11 maidens). Only celebrated Stainland batsman John Lewthwaite (24) offered much resistance. The last seven wickets fell for one run!

Golcar Pair

David Thorpe, On Both Sides of the Boundary
Peter Redding

In 1985 David Thorpe, in traditionally difficult conditions, began the season with two centuries and but for a run out may have made a third in succession. It resulted in him not speaking to Paul Scott, the other batsman involved, for two weeks! He became the first batsman that season in the Huddersfield League to pass the 500-run mark.

He played for Leymoor from 1963 to 1977 when he moved to Golcar. He was a middle-order batsman with a preference for pace bowling: "There weren't many spinners around to face." He was particularly strong when bowlers strayed onto leg stump. He was always keen to attack and this often led to his downfall: "I didn't have the concentration of a John Cooper to play long innings." He once took four wickets against Holmfirth. Asked about where he fielded, he responded "Out of the way!"

Career highlights include being a member of the Golcar team that won Section B of the 1981 Examiner 8-a-side competition and the following season he was in the side that reached the Yorkshire Champion of Champions final.

He rates Brian Turner as the best bowler he has played with and Kevin Plant as the best fielder. The best batsman is Atul Bedade. David remembers a game against Hall Bower. Prior to the match the Hall Bower players were confident of victory, so much so that a bet was agreed, £10 a player at 3/1. The Hall Bower players paid out before they even had an opportunity to bat. Bedade had clubbed an incredible 234 not out!

Facilities have improved at Golcar Cricket Club and so have the wickets "Wickets are far better at Golcar nowadays. They are more batsmen-friendly and more hundreds are scored. There isn't as much movement off the seam now as there was in years gone by when 150 or 160 would have been considered a good score."

Since his retirement in the late 1980s, David has helped out with the U11s, with auditing and fund raising and with winter tours to the Caribbean "Golcar has lost a bit of its village focus. We will never be short of players but we may be short of volunteers in the future. Will the players we have now become volunteers behind the scenes in the future?"

Mick Smith
Peter Redding

When we see high-class matches it is largely due to the surface that the game is played on. The role of the groundsman is therefore crucial. For the past decade the responsibility at Swallow Lane has fallen upon Mick Smith.

What encouraged you to become the groundsman at Golcar?

The grounds had deteriorated in the 1994 and 1995 seasons. At the start of 1996 I put myself forward for the job. I wanted to help improve the playing surface and, with the help of David Law, I think I helped to do this. I think the wickets have continued to improve since then.

Did you play cricket before you became a groundsman?

I've played cricket for Golcar all my life, starting in the U13s and progressing to be First XI captain. The highlights would be the Sykes Cup Semi-Final against Skelmanthorpe at Golcar in 1993 and then playing at Lord's in the National Indoor Finals. From a personal point of view my highlight would be the game against Dalton where I took 7 for 27, my best bowling figures. My highest score with the bat was 84 against Bradley Mills.

Has the job become easier or more difficult as time has gone on?

When I first started the equipment was old, run down and unreliable; now the mowers are newer and more reliable and this has made the job a lot easier. Although the increase in the amount of teams playing at Golcar has made me a lot busier. We now have U11 teams as well as the other age-group sides. The amount of games that the club plays increases each year, so from that point of view the job has become harder.

How do the pitches change during the course of the season?

In the early season the wickets are softer and give more help to the bowlers. As the season progresses they flatten out and become a lot harder; they are then a lot better for batting because the weather tends to intervene much less than at the start of the season.

What would you say is the ideal type of pitch?

A wicket that gives a bit of help to everyone. I think people want to see lots of runs scored. That is the way the game has been going in recent years, but you want to provide conditions that offer encouragement to the bowlers as well.

What is the most exciting match you have seen at Golcar?

The one that stands out for me is the Sykes Cup Semi-Final against Skelmanthorpe in 1993. The weather was great, there was a good crowd and it was a really great match, although unfortunately we lost by about 20 runs; it was a relatively high-scoring game so that would be my favourite match.

Two from Augustinians

Harold Ainley
Duncan Robinson

Harold Ainley is a much-loved member of Augustinians. He is a committee member and league representative, best remembered by everyone at Laund Hill for his captaincy of the First XI during the success of the 1980s, when they won either the league or the cup in 6 consecutive years. Ainley describes these years as his "best memories." Asked of his worst memory, Ainley replied "the death of one of our founder members, Michael Grimes, last year."

During his time Ainley has seen many changes, particularly the change of ground from All Saints School to the current home of Laund Hill, and the change of league from Huddersfield to the Halifax League. According to Ainley, these changes allowed the club to grow and to move forward. Ainley stressed that the committee was consistent throughout and the club remained successful and well organised.

Whilst Ainley sees the progress of the junior teams as "very positive." he concedes the club "could do with an influx of players … it's a problem but hopefully the players coming through from the junior teams will solve that."

Last summer, Ainley still captained the Second XI . When asked if he would continue playing next season his answer was "watch this space … I would love to continue playing and I don't want to stop but I've had a bad knee for a while now, and it now seems as though the other one seems to be going. I will make a decision nearer the start of the season."

Rohan Abbott: Middlesex Man Idolises Viv
Duncan Robinson

Rohan Abbott has been an invaluable member of the Augustinians set-up for two years. His first season was so successful that he was named as captain. After the highs of the first, his second proved to be anything but happy as the side struggled.

This contributed to Abbott's shock decision to leave Augustinians and retire from cricket "When you're not enjoying yourself there's no point and I'm also not getting any younger. I'm 47 now and I feel the time is right. Other clubs have tried to persuade me to come out of retirement but I'm really just looking forward to spending more time with my family."

Abbott is an aggressive right-handed batsman and his style has proved very effective in stacking up runs over the past two years. It is not only his ability with a bat that will be missed. Formerly a quick bowler, he is also a more than handy medium-fast bowler "I haven't been able to bowl as fast as I've got older."

Abbott's all-time favourite player is Viv Richards. He watched him as a youngster and what he liked most was his style and attitude and the way he "liked to dominate." He played the game for the fans and it was clear he enjoyed himself. Abbott likes to think he has a similar attitude.

Abbott, a stock controller by profession, grew up in Ilford, London. He followed Middlesex "I used to regularly attend games at Lord's because it was the nearest ground to me. Since I moved to Huddersfield eight years ago I do not really follow Middlesex as much, though." Away from the cricket field, Abbott is an accomplished musician on both piano and guitar.

Abbott says he will support the club regularly this summer "depending on the weather!" It is a shame that such a genuinely caring and down-to-earth man as Rohan Abbott has cut his playing career short.

Thurstonland Family

Joyce Booth
Toby Lock

At 12 years old, Joyce and her friends went to watch the cricketers to play *Truth, Kiss, Dare or Promise* up in the scorebox! Instead, they helped make the teas. "Teas used to be made in what is the changing room now, where the showers are. In those days, it was just a sandwich and a bun."

Joyce only ever had eyes for Geoff Booth. "Girls come down today to watch the boys play cricket; this is how they meet their boyfriends. That's exactly what happened to me. It took me 'til I was 18 to catch him, but I didn't drop him!"

So she married into the Booth family and Thurstonland Cricket Club history. Her list of jobs at the club include " ... just about everything there is in the club, I think, apart from on the field or anything to do with cricket itself! Catering mainly, bar work I'm not keen on, fund raising, selling raffle tickets, anything that really needs doing."

After Geoff's death Joyce married Ken Booth, Geoff's brother, who also played cricket for Thurstonland. The pair had three children, Andrew, Neil and Lee, all of whom play.

In 1980 Joyce joined the club committee to help fund raising. Soon she was Vice-President of the Huddersfield Arrow League, the first woman ever to hold this post. "I remember I went to the meeting as the *rep* for the club. The chairman at the time came across and said 'Excuse me, I think you've come into the wrong room.' I said, 'No actually, I've come to represent Thurstonland Cricket Club!'"

Lee Booth: Computer Genius
Toby Lock

Lee is one of seven Booths to have played for Thurstonland. He rose through the ranks as skipper in the junior teams. Nowadays, he coaches the U13 side in tandem with long-term club man Andrew Pearson.

With the Second XI, Lee averaged over 25, hit one century and took over 50 wickets in 76 games. He made his First XI debut in the early 1990s and was a regular by the mid 1990s. He took over the captaincy from long-standing skipper David Oldham and led the side to the Allsop Cup Final in 1999 and to second place in the Huddersfield Central League Premier Division in 2000.

Arguably his greatest moment came in July 2001, when, struggling at 24 for 3 away against Emley, he and batting partner John Eastwood put on a record fourth wicket partnership of 167 runs; a record that still stands.

He was the club's leading wicket-taker for three years running from 2002 to 2004, a streak that has helped him to 6th in the all-time club standings. With his current record score of 98 not out, he stands at 8th in the club's all-time run-scoring list, having bagged just under 4,000 runs for the team. Emley's run chase in the aforementioned match also saw him take his 200th First XI wicket.

Things weren't all plain sailing for Lee in 2001, though. He went on an unfortunate run of losing 12 out of 16 tosses, a record surely only matched by Michael Vaughan himself! The 2001 season also saw Thurstonland win the Huddersfield Central League Premier section for the third time in the club's history, 14 years on from their first league success.

Outside cricket, Lee is webmaster of not just the Thurstonland club site, but also the Cricket History of Calderdale and Kirklees and official Huddersfield Central Cricket League and Junior League websites.

Brother Neil is captain of the Second XI, mother Joyce is Vice-President of the Huddersfield Central Cricket League and young cousin Jack is rising through the ranks,

Thurstonland's record of always having an Oldham or Booth in the 1st XI since 1992 looks pretty safe.

Blackley Pair

Julie Pearson
Dan Barton

What is your role at Blackley Cricket Club?

I'm the club secretary but I end up doing a bit of everything. Mainly it involves sorting out the club's paperwork but it could be anything from keeping minutes at meetings to helping out with teas and catering.

How many hours a week are taken up with working at the club?

During the cricket season in summer I tend to be there for 3 to 4 hours most evenings and then all day Saturday and Sunday when matches are on. So it's quite a commitment and it's all voluntary.

How did you first get involved with working at the club?

I got involved when my husband first went to play there in 1978 and they needed a secretary so I was volunteered. Sadly my husband died in 1990 but I continued working there as I had made lots of friends at the club. I'm now in my second stint as club secretary and I've been doing it about 10 years now.

Are there any other roles women are involved in at Blackley?

Yes, we have about a dozen or so working at the club whether that be doing the teas or volunteering at fund raising events. We also have the girls that work behind the bar too.

Are girls encouraged to join the club at junior level?

We try to get as many girls along to play at junior levels. I think we have four signed on at the minute but they really only joined because their brothers played, but we would welcome any girls that want to join.

How have the male members of the club treated you?

They were all respectful towards me when I first started and because many were friends of my late husband they have supported me and respect the job I do. Some of the younger ones can be a bit cheeky but I work with men everyday in my job so I know how to deal with them.

Has your attitude to the game changed over the years?

I'd never been to a cricket match before in my life when my husband first decided to join the club but as the years have gone on, I found that I enjoy watching the cricket as well. Being part of the club is not just a social event, it's also a good sporting event to watch.

Joe Townsend
Sam Smith

How long have you been groundsman at Blackley?

I first started helping with the ground about 25 years ago, when former president Roy Chappell was the groundsman here. For the last 15 years I've been doing the majority of the work, as I'm available in the week when others are working. I do receive lots of help from people within the club and there is now a team of about six that are responsible for the ground, wickets, outfield and surrounds.

What equipment did you use in your early days?

I remember we only had one very heavy roller which took the whole team to push. So the wicket didn't get much rolling, but it did bring the team together just before the match and at the interval! We would always have a good bit of banter when rolling the wicket and it was a chance for the team to bond. The equipment was nothing like it is today and we only had one wicket mower that was handed down to us by another cricket club. In those days we even used sheep to graze on the outfield!

Do you ask the captains what kind of wicket they would like?

No, not really. We just prepare a wicket as best we can for a good game of cricket. You hear about a spinner's wicket or a batter's wicket but we haven't got the skills to do that here. We just try and create a wicket that neither favours the batters nor bowlers.

How well does the water drain at the ground?

The drainage isn't too bad at all. Up at Blackley we get strong winds that help to dry out the ground very quickly. This is not always a good thing as the wind can sometimes be too strong to play cricket! Also the strong winds prevent us from using covers. We tried using the covers on wheels but they got blown away and smashed. So our only option at the moment is to use a large plastic sheet and peg it into the ground. It's not ideal because the air can get under and it sweats, so it can still end up being damp. But it does a job if there is a short sharp shower in the middle of a game.

What future ground improvements would you like to see?

The club is certainly progressive and, although it's nothing to do with the actual playing area, we are hopefully going to have an extension on the clubhouse. The money generated from this will enable us to get better equipment that will improve the playing surface. We will be on the lookout in the market to see what equipment becomes available and generally just looking to maintain standards and improve them where we can.

Miscellany

The Sunday Cricket Debate
Brian Heywood

Sunday sport was a contentious issue in the late 1950s. Sowerby Bridge District Council had emphatically refused to open its bowling greens for Sunday use, yet leisure was beginning to encroach the Sabbath both here and on the continent.

The Halifax League was one of the first to experiment with Sunday play and it was a success. At the Mytholmroyd CC Annual General Meeting at the White Hart Hotel, Mytholmroyd, on Monday 28 October 1957, secretary ND Turner commented, "During the past season Sunday cricket has been introduced and the new venture has made a substantial increase in the club's income."

By the end of that season the club had a credit balance of £133 19s 8d.

Mount CC – Hyrstlands Park
Peter Davies

Sit up high on the banking at Hyrstlands Park, on one of the convenient benches underneath the tall, handsome trees, and admire the view. Turn left to see houses above and below. Ahead is the faded glory of Dewsbury's mills. To the right, blocks of modern, low-level flats and houses. And before you go, try and spot the Transpennine train wending its way towards Batley and Leeds or towards Huddersfield and Manchester. There may be more atmospheric cricket grounds in West Yorkshire. It may be council-owned. But it is home.

Drawing by Sue Brant

Mount began their tenancy in 1977. Clubs based in charming rural areas, like the Holme Valley or the Calder Valley, have a straightforward challenge to exist. Urban clubs (North Kirklees is predominantly urban and industrial) have a plethora of issues to contend with: finding a spare parcel of green land, vandalism, dog-walkers who do not respect the sanctity of sports grounds and general upkeep and maintenance.

The club has played at other venues, including Pontefract Racecourse of all places, and other clubs have used Hyrstlands. But the park, high above Batley Carr, remains of central importance. Mount have a long-term arrangement with the local council and have played here for most of their thirty odd years.

Wander into the park, into an amazing sporting amphitheatre. The banking gives the ground a special feel just like The Hill at Sydney. Every weekend, loyal spectators sit on the bank, or on the benches at the top where you can not only see the cricket, but you can also enjoy the spectacular North Kirklees panorama. Players and spectators also gather by the clubhouse. Keen Mount youngsters sit attentively in front, scoring and updating the portable scoreboard. It's not called Mount and Mount Pleasant for nothing.

The club's vision is ambitious. To stay at Hyrstlands because of its symbolic importance, but also to develop and level the field and con-struct a new changing-room block. They are negotiating with Kirklees officials and other stakeholders and the exposure they are gaining this summer on Sky TV will help.

My Father and Spen Victoria
Jean Margetts

I was brought up to be very interested in cricket as my father was a good player and took a keen interest in watching it on TV. His name was Frederick Anthony Margetts, Tony to everyone, and he played at Leeds University before the war. We lived in Birkenshaw and he taught at Gomersal County School, afterwards Gomersal Middle, for years, and coached cricket and football all the time. I remember a Peter Booth? who went on to play for Yorkshire being at school. I used to go along to the after-school practices sometimes.

My dad was very devoted to sport at school and used to go off to all the inter-school matches and was part of a Spen Valley schools sports group that used to meet in a pub in Cleckheaton, the *Wilton*, I think, at the bottom of Spen Bank as you come into Cleckheaton. He also used to be active at *Cleck* Rugby club and I can remember going with him to mark out the lines at Rawfolds with some white stuff and then he filled up the big bath. As an older man he used to go to Spen Victoria Cricket Club bar every week but I'm not sure if he did any coaching.

My dad once took me to see Yorkshire play in Bradford when Fred Trueman was bowling but I was a bit young to understand much

Cricket Bats
Lee Hughes (Ms)

Modern advances in sporting designs
create brand new bats with meticulous lines
Gone are the days of addressing the call
armed with no more than a stick and a ball

Cricket's been dragged to a technical age
where designer precision is now all the rage
Action grip handles increase shock control
ensuring full power that crucifies all

Contoured and shaped with extravagant spines
in a Kashmir or English willow that shines
Handles now tapered with Graphite inside
enhances the sweetspot increasing the slide

Utterly tested so performance will last
A lifetime success can be almost forecast
But a masterpiece crafted with insight and vision
is entirely redundant if not used with precision

.

In the Fast Lane
David Brenchley

Cricket is, conventionally, a quiet sport, unless you play for, or against, Outlane Cricket Club. In 1970, the club's ground, where they had played since the 1930s, was affected by the building of a new motorway between Liverpool and Hull.

The M62 was mooted in 1962 and the route finally chosen went right through the club's square and Outlane unsuccessfully objected to its building. They were compensated to the tune of around £2,000, according to club treasurer Andrew Wray. £1,800 of this was needed to re-create the pitch after the motorway was completed.

During the time it took them to build the motorway, the club had to up sticks but found it difficult to purchase land. Wray said "We tried to move but people wouldn't sell. Farmers were reluctant because they were terrified that it was for development and they wouldn't get much money for it." In the end, the field was pushed right onto the edge of Lindley Moor and the club moved to Highfields, just outside Huddersfield town centre.

Wray said:

We went back at the start of the 1974 season, which coincided with our departure from the Huddersfield Cricket Association and our entry into the Halifax Cricket League. As you would imagine, there are frequently complaints about the noise coming from the motorway, especially when umpires fail to hear little nicks from the batsmen. At both ends of the ground you get trouble; at the top end it is noisier whereas at the bottom end you are looking directly at the passing cars.

Club veteran Trevor Crosland explains "A lot of people mention the noise but you get used to it. We put all these trees down to try and blank it off a bit."

Wray remembers a story from when he played for the club "[I was playing with] a lad called Malcolm Blackburn and he said, 'is this traffic bothering you?'" Wray had got used to the motorway by that point and admitted that it didn't bother him. He continued: "[Blackburn then] said, 'I've just been watching that wagon go up the motorway and I couldn't take my eyes off it!' Most people get on with it but it does affect a few." Nowadays, however "it is a far bigger factor than in 1974 because there is an awful lot more traffic."

My Dad
Peter Davies

My Dad strode out to bat, without pads or gloves. It was the early 1970s. He was playing in a cricket match within the grounds of the local hospital. He was chaplain at the hospital and I was there to watch from the boundary edge. I was sat at long stop or very straight long-on/long-off, depending on which end the bowling was coming from.

He had promised me before the match that he would try and hit a six. He delivered too. It was a straightish shot which ballooned over long-on. I saw it from behind. It was a swashbuckling effort. I could feel the force and power of it from the boundary. The fact that he did it against fast bowling (when you're young, all bowlers look fast) and didn't wear pads or gloves, and he had hit a proper cricket ball (a bright red *corky*) was even more impressive. My Dad had hit the six he had promised me and I was in awe of him.

The hospital was not just any hospital. We lived in Culcheth, a small village situated halfway between Leigh and Warrington in north Cheshire. The hospital was called Newchurch, or the *Mental Hospital*. Villagers, and especially me and my friends at the local school, talked about the place in a jocular way. We were young and political correctness was a long way off. It was the local *madhouse* and jokes about it were ten-a-penny at school. My Dad, as the local Methodist minister, was the chaplain, and he had obviously received a special invite to play in the cricket match. I can't remember whether it was *Staff v Patients* or two mixed sides playing each other, or maybe there was some other arrangement. (I am told that once upon a time it was quite normal for asylums and psychiatric hospitals to arrange cricket matches for patients; it was a form of therapy, to let them out and to encourage them to run around and get some fresh air).

I think my Dad got out soon after hitting the six, ending up with maybe 8, 10 or 13 runs to his name. Perhaps this was the first organised cricket match I ever attended.

I have some very vivid memories of my early years, and many revolve around sport. There was my Dad's six, the shopping trip to Warrington with my Mum to buy a new *Subbuteo* soccer team, collecting football stickers, and the Saturday afternoons sat in front of TV watching live rugby league, with Eddie Waring providing the commentary. In those days, cricket competed with football for my affections. It was very much fifty-fifty then. Over the decades that followed I've become primarily a cricket lover.

Culcheth was a fairly ordinary place. There was a mix of council housing and posh new residences, and an old-style village green in the centre. The only remarkable thing about Culcheth was the Methodist church; a spectacular modern building where my Dad was the minister. We lived next door.

My Dad, obviously, was a major influence. We played cricket in the back garden and the driveway. He always bowled underarm spin, had a formidably safe pair of hands, and batted in correct, orthodox fashion. We also played *Owzat* in the lounge. It was a hit. We would play the game endlessly, rolling the two dice-like *rollers* from dawn until dusk (though I have particular memories of playing the game in early evening; maybe the last thing we did before we had to go to bed). We would invent XIs to play against each other (England v Rest of the World, Australia v West Indies) and we would also mix in the names of family members and friends. Two small *rollers* never brought a household so much fun.

My Dad was actually quite ingenious in the games he played with us. There was *Owzat*, but also an exciting game where 32 pieces of paper were placed in a hat, each with a football team's name on. The teams were drawn out in pairs, and then we would put a set of numbers in the hat and draw these out so that each match had a scoreline. We'd do this until there was a *Cup Final*, and a victor would eventually emerge.

Integration and Equal Opportunities
Sam Christie

The number of people from ethnic minorities living in Huddersfield and West Yorkshire has risen significantly over the last 30 years, benefiting many of the area's cricket teams, including Bradley & Colnebridge.

Ethnic players have made such a huge impact that the club's chairman and groundsman, Raymond Hawkyard has said "There's no doubt

without our four or five regular ethnic players we would have folded a long time ago."

The biggest influx occurred during the 1970s when immigrants moved to England in search of more prosperous jobs and improved living conditions. Raymond Hawkyard remembers "There weren't any ethnic minority players at the club until the 1980s. The first three players to join Bradley & Colnebridge were three West Indian lads called Joe Cyras, Ray Reid and Chris Fullerton. They all knew each other from school and were also friends with my nephew who told them to come down."

Hawkyard states "It's only been over the last three or four years that a large number of Asians have joined the club. A lot of them know each other and invite their friends down."

League Representative and Sponsorship Secretary Steve Ashwell has also overseen the changes. About some Asian cricketers "There's no doubt we benefit from the good players but they don't really join in with the social aspect of the cricket club. They certainly enjoy their cricket but they like to turn up, play the match, then go, which is similar to many cricket clubs in Huddersfield. They don't spend money on drink after the match and gamble like a lot of the other lads. We accept and respect their culture and do our best to integrate them into our club."

One significant *barrier,* according to Hawkyard, is the differences in language "I try to encourage them to integrate but they don't mix like they should do. They don't all speak English and sometimes break off into groups and speak their own languages. Despite this they still manage to communicate well in training and in matches."

Hawkyard outlines club policy:

I don't have a problem with ethnic minorities who live locally joining the club. It would annoy me if we decided to pay one of the club's players to compete for the club. My wife Barbara works very hard and raises in the region of £1,000 a year on tea money and I wouldn't want this to be spent on a player's wages. There are too many overseas players competing in local cricket nowadays. Our club is about giving everybody a game no matter how good they are. We don't want our club to be similar to Arsenal in football where there are now very few British-based players.

We're Going to Barbados!
Brian Heywood

Golcar Cricket Club first toured Barbados prior to the 1992 season. A link was made with the North Stars Club who arranged a six match tour around the northern part of the island.

Whilst there, the party met former Worcestershire and Barbados fast bowler Hartley Alleyne. Hartley had considerable experience of league cricket in northern England, having helped Haslingden to two Lancashire League titles between 1983 and 1986. He also played for Colne and Walsden, amongst others. Married to a Todmorden girl, Hartley was planning to return to England as an overseas amateur for Walsden in 1993 but was persuaded to play as Golcar's professional instead.

With Hartley's assistance, Golcar's visits to Barbados became bi-annual affairs. The club has enjoyed the privilege of playing against some of the island's best cricketers, including Collis King and Franklyn Stephenson.

The North Stars Club is thriving and their ground is now used for first class cricket. In 2004 the club had the honour of hosting the final of the Carib Trophy.

Golcar's links with the island were further strengthened when Hartley Alleyne brought a team from Barbados to play a friendly match at Golcar in 2004.

The club's international connections have been extended by Atul Bedade, Golcar's Indian professional from 1999 to 2004. Through him several Indian touring teams have played friendly matches at the ground.

Multiculturalism
Peter Davies and Rob Light

Kirklees has sizeable Asian and African-Caribbean communities and cricket has always been an important vehicle for mixing the cultures. It

Solly

started with black professionals like Edwin Hill coming to Slaithwaite in the 1930s. It continued with the arrival of Asian and West Indian professionals when Second World War improvements in aircraft design opened up long-haul routes. Suddenly, clubs had the ability to sign professional cricketers from the Caribbean and the Subcontinent, and they in turn could make a name for themselves in the northern leagues, and earn some money.

They were part of wider post-war immigration when families travelled to Britain in search of a better life and an improved standard of living. Many settled in the North where industrial towns like Huddersfield, Dewsbury and Batley were seeking additional workers.

Asians worked in the textile industry, W Indians in public transport. They established their own cricket clubs. Whilst they were not *exclusive*, they were distinct organisations, serving the specific cultural and language needs of first generation immigrants. One immigrant recalls:

There were no Asian cricketers. I'd go to practise and turn up to the match and I'd always be the twelfth man. If they were a man short I'd be slotted in, but even though they knew I could bat, I'd go in at number 10 or 11. It was a waste of time, basically, so we used to play in the street with a tennis ball but one day I thought this can't go on, we've got to do something about it.

Stanley Inniss arrived in Huddersfield from the Caribbean in the 1950s and became a stalwart of local league cricket. He remembers: "When I came I was accepted because I was a good cricketer. A good many of my friends who had not been accepted had a lot of problems. In the end some of them decided to go back home."

It is now common for cricket clubs' constitutions to include references to the battle against racism. There are Asian Restaurants who sponsor Kirklees cricket clubs. A number of Kirklees Asian boys have played for Yorkshire. But perhaps the most powerful evidence for cricket as an agent for integration in Kirklees is embodied by Solly Adam. A Muslim Indian who came to West Yorkshire in the 1960s from the troubled province of Gujarat near Bombay. He started his cricketing career at Batley Muslims CC and went on to play for a variety of clubs, including Batley, Cleckheaton and Spen Victoria. Adam is also a businessman. He owns petrol stations with his brother and has established his own sports shop, Solly Sports. He is nicknamed *Mr Cricket* and acted as agent in the deal between Sachin Tendulkar and Yorkshire. Before that, he took Imran Khan to Wakefield. Tendulkar stayed at Adam's house for three months in 1990. "A very nice boy" Adam recalls. "Very humble and down to earth. In my view he's the best ever but then, I didn't see Bradman."

Adam also sponsors *The Press Top 20 Solly Sports Awards*, which are designed to give recognition to local players and officials of the 20 senior league clubs in the Batley-Dewsbury area. Adam, together with The Press Sports staff, comprise a special panel which selects *The Young Player of the Year*, *The Team of the Year* and *The Special Merit Award for Services to Local Cricket*. Adam is also involved in a new project backed by the Prince's Trust and *NatWest* which links teams of disadvantaged young people with first-class county cricket clubs to help

16-25 year olds develop the skills and confidence they need to realise their potential:

> To see an Asian playing for Yorkshire would give me pleasure, and I think the time is coming when it will be normal for them to play for Yorkshire, and then normal to play for England. There's no way they can stop that now. At the end of the day, your heart and soul must be in the country where you're born and bred, and where you're going to live all your life. I love to see Asians born and bred here support England. Like my wife always says, a garden always looks nicer if there are different coloured roses.

And Stanley Inniss? He's an MBE, magistrate and chairman of the Kirklees Racial Equality Council.

Flyn
(My son the cricketer part I)
David Walker

In the nineteen-nineties, on Summer Sunday mornings, my son Chris played on the all-weather pitch for the local U13s. Practice was Tuesday evenings. However inclement, Flyn was down the club to teach, encourage, organise and umpire. In the winter he took us all to the Yorkshire indoor nets. A cathedral-like space of hush and respect. Until Yorkshire Ladies arrived.

In his fifties, Flyn was tall, slim, balding with rimless spectacles. His spare frame, simple white sweater and track suit bottoms gave him a monk-like appearance. He had his dark side, which we never saw. Though I tell a lie. I did once call unannounced at his home. Lesley, his wife, answered. She worked from home whilst Flyn was in and out of jobs. No, Flyn wasn't around, could she deal with it? "Of course," I said. In the shadows I glimpsed two small round spots of light. They must have been around five foot ten. Unnerving, peering back at me out of the gloom.

Flyn was never cross, except with his own lads, Dean and Rick.

Lesley said she and Flyn kept them permanently on the move, off the streets, "Dean's the youngest with the attitude. Poor Rick's feet never touch the ground. Cricket three and four nights a week, and he's grown five inches this year. Plays havoc with his knees."

Every year, during the school holidays, Barnsley CC hosted an U13 six-a-side knockout competition and Flyn had entered us. The forecast was poor as we set out for the deep south. A three vehicle convoy and a squad of nine …

Barnsley Cricket Club, Shaw Road. A working men's club at mid-wicket, barred and closed with a sign on the door that said *members only*. Crumpled coloured metallic paper litter blowing across the out-field. Thick ropes marking a boundary with wasteland beyond. Derelict corrugated shed roofs for covers. Grim under grey dismal skies. Welcome.

"Is this the real Barnsley Cricket Club? Home of Parkinson and others?" I asked. Flyn said yes.

There was a tea-bar next to the labour club with a warning sign! "Do not enter Saturdays mornings between 9.30 am and midday: *Archery Club* practice." We went in gingerly. A long narrow room with multicoloured targets in the distance. Grey walls, grey formica-topped tables, grey chairs and a wet floor. Three ladies served bags of sweets and crisps, cans of pop, grey mugs of hot brown water and bacon sandwiches. No bows and arrows.

Flyn had checked the order of play, "We'll have to keep the lads occupied. I'll do a few routines with them. Let's have something to eat first."

We sat on the boundary, watching with cans and sandwiches. Small crowd, most noise from the pitch. Rick, Reg and Shane were the senior players. Tall, seasoned 13 year olds. They will shoulder the responsibility of the last overs. Mike, Simon, Chris and Dean were somewhere in the middle, fiery and gobby. Gareth, Tom and Joe, the youngsters, eight and nine year olds, just about taller than a full-size bat.

I went round with a black plastic bag as they sauntered off to practice behind the tea-bar.

Then we were on. "Come on lads, get your pads on," said Flyn. Everyone batted and bowled. 10 overs, start with 200, 2 for a wide except in the last over, 8 knocked off for a wicket. Short cover and midwicket boundaries. They gave us thirty odd in extras and we only had 2 down, one a run out. We finished with 268. Strange we didn't turn straight round, just when we were feeling good. Another two teams batted and fielded before we tried to bowl our lot out.

The grey overcast cloud turned into steady rain. Our turn to field. Reg's over was expensive. So was Chris's. No wides from us but their first two batters did well. And suddenly our lads were all having a go at each other. Flyn got them in a huddle at the end of the third over. Gave them a talking to. Then it was back to normal.

Last 2 overs and they needed 24 to win. Tight. Last over and 14 to win. Reg had the responsibility, made up for his first. They were 4 short at the finish, good fielding, no overthrows and no wides. A man with a Barnsley accent and a microphone sat behind a window at the tea bar and summarised the scores after each over. "Most exciting match yet," he said. The small crowd clapped, and the boys, red faced and smiling, walked to the car park.

"Flyn has done well today, Lesley," I said.

"You should see him when he's not on view."

Second game against Barnsley and they were all Rick-sized, even a girl with the pony tail. They batted first. We kept the wides down, fielded and backed up well, but they still scored 280. Again a break for two other teams to play. Our turn to bat and we could not keep the score going against good length bowling. All off long runs, even the girl with the pony tail. We didn't lose wickets, but we didn't get runs either. Until hero Rick stepped to the wicket, supported by younger brother Dean. Square drives and hearty pulls. Flyn had told them to play shots. A spectacular finale and the right result. Home team winners and the crowd slightly more animated. No complaints from our lads.

It was still throwing it down as we gathered in the car park and sorted whose kit went where and who was taking who home. I couldn't see Flyn, until I looked over to the minibus. He sat staring through the windscreen. Steady yet fragile. Tolerant yet capable of mild censure: a tired smile, a *tut* and a shake of the head. You had to smarten up somehow.

I haven't seen much of Flyn since. He was a big reason why Chris was cricket daft.

Married to Cricket

Hilary Holmes
Muni Rashid

How did you become involved with the club?

Well I became secretary of Linthwaite in about 1991 or 1992; sorry I can't remember the exact year! My husband and son played cricket and I used to go and support them and I guess things progressed from there! My first job was as a tea lady at Emley CC and it has progressed from there. To be honest though I have been brought up with cricket since I was about two years old, my family were involved in cricket. One way of putting it is that cricket has been drilled in to me since childhood! Just like today you see families who are obsessed with football, well for me and my family it was cricket.

How do the male members of the club treat you?

They treat me very well, they always have done. There has not been much female input at the club. I mean most of the men at the club are married to the sport! So they welcome any females at the club! At the moment we have a young tea lady and everyone gets on very well with her.

Are there any other roles that women play at your club?

Well, besides the tea lady it is a hugely male-populated environment. We do have a bowling club too and we have men's and women's bowling teams. This creates a good atmosphere among the teams and a sense of togetherness. Although a lot of mothers, wives and girlfriends come and offer their support, unfortunately that is as far as it goes.

How involved are ethnic minorities at your club?

We are a mixed group of people. Just last week a West Indian professional (Deighton Butler) arrived at the club and he has mixed in very well with the others. We are also involved with ethnic minorities on the social side. For example we have toured Barbados and Australia and met some very lovely people, and in return they have come to stay with us at Linthwaite.

Sue Woolford
Gareth Thompson

What is your role within Luddenden Cricket Club?

My role at the club now is simply as a scorer. I am retired from the secretary's job but I still attend committee meetings. I felt I needed a break after so many years as a volunteer at the cricket club although I am still very much involved.

What was your job when you were secretary?

My job meant I was responsible for many parts of the club's general running. I was responsible for committee meetings and keeping the minutes there. There were administrative requirements and I also had to return the averages. I still did the scoring.

Did you enjoy the work?

It was not a case of enjoying the job; it was always a case for waiting for a problem. One of the major problems came with converting the old licence of the bar to a new licence, which involved a lot of work. My legal background came in very handy for the job. This took place in 2004/5.

How did you get involved with the club?

I started off by going to the ground occasionally and I was asked to help with auditing the accounts and help to raise a grant for the pavilion and an extension for the ground. After that, I was then voted in as club secretary. Basically it came about because my brother's father-in-law used to play and you just get to know people.

Are there any other roles that women play at your club?

At the moment the First and Second team scorers are women and for a year or two I dealt with the bar accounts. All the work at the club is purely voluntary work. The work of the tea ladies is very helpful particularly at junior level where the ladies would turn up and help with refreshments.

Shelf Women's Committee
David Febrero

The England Women's 2005 Ashes victory, although overshadowed by the men's triumph over the Aussies, was great for the recognition of women's cricket at a local and national level. Or so one would have thought. At Shelf, and other similar clubs, women's cricket is non-existent.

For many years, Shelf's women have provided tea on match days and organised fund raisers. "We did a lot of bring-and-buy sales and sponsored walks and things," ex-ladies committee member Carol Boardall said. "We formed it solely for money-making purposes; although we didn't make much initially, we did contribute to the club."

Carol kept a log of the money raised. "In 1975 the second team raised £3.30 and the first team raised £3.14. You couldn't get much for that nowadays of course," she admits. They often baked and prepared food themselves in order to maximise profits.

Drawing by Sue Brant

"We have thought about re-establishing the committee," Carol declared. "But it is a different world now; we had 10 women at one point but nowadays nobody can find the time to form a committee, and if we formed our own cricket team we wouldn't be the best side in the world to watch!" Once upon a time a Shelf women's team played a friendly against the Shelf men's first team, an experience that was rather humbling. "That was a funny game. It was a close one, I think we only just lost it," Carol joked.

20th Century (2)

Interlude - II
The Final that Took Weeks and Weekes Disaster
Allan Stuttard

On Wood Cup Semi-Final day, Walsden scored 151 for 6 and skittled Milnrow for 111. Weekes scored 58 and took 3 for 50. Walsden were now in the final for only the second time in their long history, against Middleton the then current league leaders.

Disaster struck when Wardle was pronounced fit and Ronnie Wood returned as club professional. There was no Sunday cricket then and all cup games took place midweek, hence the Final was due to start Monday evening 26 July at Rochdale. During the prior Saturday league game Ronnie got injured. It's not clear why or how, but he bowled unchanged throughout and it has been suggested someone trod on his foot. The Chairman and *Wilty* stumped up yet again and Everton DeCourcy Weekes was engaged for a third time as deputy pro.

It rained all week. They tried again the following week when it continued to rain, during which, it is alleged, Weekes lost a large proportion of his fee in a card game.

4 - Twenty-First Century

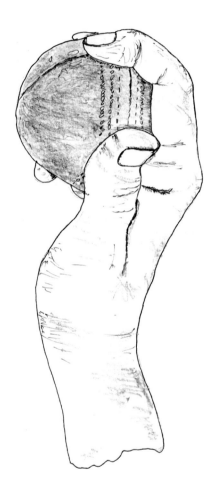

Drawing by Clive Hetherington

Achievement

125 years of hurt are ended
Peter Redding

Honley Cricket Club celebrated its 125 year anniversary as the 2005 season began, with one thing outstanding. They still hadn't won a Drakes Premiership title in the Huddersfield and District League.

Honley had long been established as a Premiership side. They were boosted by the presence of a number of professional first class cricketers. In addition they had recruited a number of players from their successful rivals Thongsbridge. Simon Kelly, Danny Howard, Richard Jakeman, Richie Howarth and Simon England had all been brought in from a club that had been stronger than Honley for all of the 1990s. Not only did these players have considerable ability they also had what Club Secretary Tim Hirst calls the "winning mentality that was needed at the club."

August 7, the date of The Romida Sykes Cup Final, was the beginning of the success story. Honley had a only won the Sykes Cup once in eight attempts. Their opponents were Delph & Dobcross who were making their debut in the Final. Their team included former Lancashire paceman Mike Smethurst, who had played county cricket up until a couple of years prior to 2005. Honley lost the toss and were put in to bat by Delph captain Grant Jones. For once the reliable opening combination of Simon Kelly and Danny Howard was breached early. This cleared the stage for Richard Jakeman to hit 95 and Steve Crook 50 as Honley recorded a strong total of 251 for 6. All of Honley's bowlers then chipped in with important wickets as Delph & Dobcross were restricted to just 155. Ritchie Howarth was the pick, taking 4 for 47. Steve Crook, Martin Green and Rajesh Pawar all took two apiece. Richard Jakeman was named as the man of the match. Honley were presented with the Cup by Bruce Jakeman, father of Richard, who was in the Honley side that won in 1982. Could the Sykes Cup win provide Honley with the inspiration they needed to finally capture their first Drakes Huddersfield & District League Championship?

Honley's 2005 successes can be put down to many things but it was the club's professionals that provided the telling contributions. Steve Crook of Lancashire, spearhead of the bowling attack, took 58 wickets. His aggressive middle order batting was also vital. They were also aided by the services of Yorkshire batsman Matthew Wood. The overseas professional was Rajesh Pawar, a left arm spinner

who has played first class cricket in India for Mumbai. With 82 wickets, Pawar was the club's leading bowler. It was noticeable that when both Crook and Pawar were unavailable for the last three matches, Honley struggled. They were comfortably placed at the top of the League when they suffered back-to-back defeats against Meltham and Golcar, setting up a tense finale away at Kirkburton. Surely Honley wouldn't throw away the League title at the final hurdle? It ended a non-event with Yorkshire's famous cricketing weather making play impossible at any of the scheduled matches. At last Honley could toast their first Drakes Byrom Huddersfield & District League Championship.

Honley had led for most of the season and Club Secretary Tim Hirst singled out openers Simon Kelly and Danny Howard for praise for their role in getting the club into this position "They have been great all year in scoring about 2,000 runs between them. This has always given us good starts for the batsmen to build on." Hirst also praised Captain Rob Moore calling him the "Mike Brearley of the team." Moore commented "It was Honley's 125th Anniversary this summer, so it was quite fitting that we should capture the Championship for the first time."

Honley were also awarded the Huddersfield Examiner's *Sports Team of the Year* for what was a historic double of League Championship and Sykes Cup.

Queens Road Muslims
Peter Davies

This is a remarkable cricket team. QRM started out in 1974 as a group of teenagers eager to do something constructive with their spare time. In 2004 they stand as the superpower of the Halifax Association.

Young Asian men, trying to get along in the most *English* of sports, after 25 years of league combat, have moved from isolation to inte-

gration. An urban cricket team, based in the back streets of downtown Halifax, they cannot hire their own ground and have had their applications to join the Halifax League rebuffed. So desperate have they been to move out of the old amateur league that in recent years they have considered merger.

According to the Halifax census, 93 per cent of the population is white and approximately 5.7 per cent of Asian extraction (which amounts to almost 11,000). According to John Hargreaves, author of the 1999 book *Halifax*, most first-generation immigrants came over from Kashmircl "seeking night-shift employment in local textile mills in the 1950s." More accurately, these migrants came from Mirpur and North Punjab. Asian players turn out for a variety of Halifax League & Association outfits and, but for the odd *racist incident*, there is widespread harmony and integration.

QRM are a first-rate amateur cricket team (their list of honours demonstrates this) but they are not just a cricket team. They are a community of Asians, Muslims and friends. Several elder statesmen of the side have made a career in the world of social work. Initially, QRM were a kind of unofficial youth club, and the bonds that were created were strong and long lasting. Today the nearest thing they have to a base is the British Muslim Association, a day-care centre located at the junction of Hopwood Lane and Queen's Road.

The teenagers who created the club in 1974 are still neighbours and pals in 2004. For example, Najabat works for Calderdale Council at Raven Street Youth and Community Centre, while next door Mushtaq Mohammed, a seasoned mechanic, repairs clapped-out vehicles in the garage that he owns. Cricket helped this group of young Asians to mature and make a path for themselves in life. QRM have become a *club* in an informal and spontaneous way and have dispensed with the formal bureaucracy associated with many local cricket clubs. This has frustrated local cricket administrators, but it has enabled the team to enjoy themselves in the way they have wanted to.

Clubmark & New Nets
David Brenchley

Outlane Cricket Club had a double celebration this week. They were presented with their Clubmark certificate from the English Cricket Board and also opened their new double-net facility.

The Clubmark presentation was made by Steve Archer, Cricket Development Officer for the Yorkshire County Cricket Board, who said, "I can't emphasise how much work has gone into this and what it will mean for [the club's] future development."

The nets, at a cost of £20,000, were funded through the National Lottery's *Awards for All* Scheme, who donated £10,000. Other contributors were the Lord's Taverners (£3,000), Kirklees Local Area Committee, through local councillor Tony Brice (£2,000), Holme Valley Lodge (£1,000) and Calderdale Community Foundation (£1,000).

Outlane Chairman Anthony Briggs said, "It is a magnificent achievement for a small club like ourselves. We are very grateful for all the help and contributions we have received."

David Normanton, President of the Halifax Cricket League, congratulated the Huddersfield-based club which runs two Saturday teams, a Sunday league team and four junior teams.

MBE Honour!
Sam Hollis

Holmfirth CC can proudly announce that Head Coach Tony Eustance has been awarded the MBE in the Queen's Birthday Honours List.

Tony has been working with young people in sport for nearly 50 years as a teacher and sports coach. The nomination for the honour came from former colleagues, parents and pupils from the schools where he taught in Liverpool and Chester. The much respected coach now lives and works in Holmfirth. Tony was instrumental in forming Liverpool-based Oulton Park's impressive junior section, but started his teaching career in Toxteth in 1961. For many years he worked at Parklands School in Speke, where he taught English, Drama and, of course, cricket. From 1991 to 2002, Tony was based in Cheshire, where he worked with people of all ages in cricket, from county squads to handicapped teams, and with all ages from 4 years to 70.

Tony retired from teaching five years ago and moved with his wife Irene to the Holme Valley. It did not take him long to link up with Holmfirth Cricket Club, and it is largely through Tony's drive and enthusiasm that the club is expanding its junior set-up so effectively. "I'm absolutely delighted," Tony said of the award, "not only have I enjoyed every single moment in the game of cricket, I've got paid too!"

(Birthday Honours List June 2008 - Anthony Eustance. For services to Education and to Young People in Liverpool and Cheshire).

Dave Fletcher
Ian Hirst

Dave Fletcher maintains the cricket and football fields at Hullen Edge Road, Elland. The venue was once part of the Savile Estate and covers eight acres of land.

Elland is renowned in the Huddersfield League as a batsman's paradise with big scores always on the agenda. Fletcher won the FE Greenwood Trophy for the best maintained ground in the League in 2003.

Add that to his West Riding Football Association medallion for the best football pitch and the Huddersfield Bowling Association award for the best bowling green.

On a match day, during tea, when everyone is tucking into the sandwiches, Fletcher and his group of helpers are in the middle doing their stuff. First, the loose grass and dust is brushed away from the batsman's crease so that the bowlers will not injure themselves as they arrive at the popping crease. The batting crease can be re-marked by placing a long piece of straight wood along the lines and paint along it. A roller is  also brought in to flatten the pitch so that the wicket remains even for both sides. The only thing they cannot control is the weather.

After the game the covers are brought on to cover next week's wicket. The elements are uncontrollable so the covers keep the pitch dry and the drainage system (on the covers) helps filter the water away from the wicket and onto the outfield. One of the hardest jobs for the groundsman is moving the covers. The size of those at Elland means you certainly keep fit.

Being a groundsman has now become a specialist art form. There are dedicated websites that give advice to groundstaff about what they should be doing during each month of the season. One of these is www.pitchcare.com. The website gives details of courses and colleges. It keeps groundsmen up to date with the latest information and equipment that is available to maintain the perfect cricket pitch.

Professionals

Steve Whitwam
Peter Redding

Steve Whitwam has been the most influential Golcar player over the past two seasons. In 2005 and 2006, he gained back-to-back best all-rounder titles as Golcar secured top-half positions in the Huddersfield Premier League. He swapped Golcar for Scholes for the 2001 season to play premier division cricket, returning to Golcar in 2005 when they had won promotion. He made a century in his comeback match against Kexborough.

Steve is a free-scoring left-handed batsman who also has strong powers of concentration and a solid temperament. He was the first man to make 500 runs in the Huddersfield League in 2005.

Cobber, as he is known by his Golcar teammates, is also an intelligent off-spin bowler. He has good control of line and length, sustainable over long spells, cleverly using the slight slope that is often talked about at Swallow Lane to exaggerate turn. "My weakness is I try to bowl players out when I get frustrated rather than tie them down and wait for a mistake." Reliable slip-catching skills make him the complete all-rounder.

Steve arrived from Melbourne, Australia, as a 13 year old, having played for Melbourne club, Coomoora, at the age of 8. He was the most promising junior in the Huddersfield League and made his maiden century for Golcar Firsts against Kexborough at the age of 16.

Sledging is quite rare in the League but Steve says he looks forward to it:

Grade cricket in Australia is much different to club cricket in England. The standard in Australia is very tough. They sledge and bounce you a lot more and they are not as friendly as in England. I got sledged more in Australia when I was 10 than I do now in England. I also think there is a lack of specialist coaching in England, whereas in Australia coaching is seen as vital at any level.

Whitwam spent a brief period with Northamptonshire Seconds. "I regret not trying my luck with another county after Northants let me go."

Wasim Jaffer
Michael Ward

In 2001 Wasim Jaffer scored 1,379 runs at an average of 100 for Scholes in the Huddersfield League. Former captain Paul Wharton, describes him as "the finest cricketer I have ever seen in league cricket; and that includes county men, overseas players, the lot. He is incredible."

Wasim Jaffer started his career as an 18 year old in 1996/97 with Mumbai. He scored an incredible triple century in only his second First Class match, breaking Mumbai's record for an away individual score. Jaffer made his Test debut for India against South Africa in 2000. He was, however, unable to cope with an experienced South African attack, scoring just 46 runs in his four innings.

Two years later he had the chance to atone and will remember India's tour of the West Indies. His highest score of 86 in Antigua ensured his place on the next tour of England. Yet again Jaffer's form deserted him at a crucial time and he was dropped after two Tests. Another three-year break followed but his excellent club form could not be ignored. He made the side to play against the England tourists and made his first century for India in the first game.

Jaffer cemented his place in India's Test team by becoming India's second highest scorer in the West Indies in the next series. His mammoth 212 against Antigua was enough to earn him a central contract, seemingly confirming him as one of the first-choice opening batsmen.

Top Amateurs

Rick Lunn: The World of Captaincy
Paul Rai

Armitage Bridge CC had a tough season in 2006 finishing bottom. A change was required to get the *Bridge* firing again and 25 year old Rick Lunn was the man for the job. Fresh innovative ideas and Lunn's cricket brain helped him command respect. According to Lunn, being a teacher benefited his captaincy: "organisation, delegation and speaking to people in the right way. Treating people as individuals is essential to build a rapport."

Lunn admits the transition to captain wasn't that easy. It tends to divert attention from the basics of the game, like playing every delivery on its

merits. A captain's mind can stray when out in the middle as it is he who has a million thoughts running through his head: "In some games we really needed a captain's innings and I bottled it; I was thinking too much." Lunn recalled an occasion out in the middle against Broad Oak: "I faced four balls and looked like I had never batted before. Fortunately we went on to win the game." When asked whether the captaincy had any positive effects on his personal performance he laughingly said, "Yes. My best ever bowling figures of 4 for 31." Despite injury to his back in pre-season preventing him from bowling to full capacity.

There is a school of thought that believes bowlers do not make good captains. Lunn agrees "I'm a bowler by trade; it was easier captaining without having to bowl. I've always said bowlers shouldn't be captains."

In his debut season they finished a respectable fifth in the League.

Lunn highlights the squad as the main factor: "Nine or ten players scored a fifty; everyone chipped in and contributed. We wouldn't have finished fifth if it weren't for the contributions from everyone."

Some say a captain is only as good as his team, but the decisions made by a captain can have a say on the outcome of a match. Lunn echoed this opinion "As a captain you can have a big impact on the game with bowling and fielding changes. Against Paddock at home they were going nowhere slowly with 50 for 4 in 35 overs, we had 200 plus on the board and we needed all the points, so I crowded the bat and they didn't know what to do."

Relationships with players can change once someone becomes captain. Selection can be an extremely tough task for a captain. Lunn said, "The hardest thing I had to do was drop Mike Webb. He has been at the club for a long time and is a legend; he is a real club character." Lunn explained the reason for leaving a bowler on for slightly longer than expected "It's the fast bowlers union; when I'm taken off early as a bowler and I'm down at third man or fine leg, I think I should still be bowling. I'm giving the bowler the opportunity and I'm backing him." Lunn went on to say "The hardest thing is keeping everyone happy. Trying not to favour friends and ignore others. It's also improved some relationships, because you have to speak to more people, you go up to people and say I think this, what do think about this?"

Lunn had the assistance of the first ever overseas professional: "It's a massive benefit; he lifts everybody. He brings your game along, with hints and tips. He'll have ideas other people wouldn't."

Rick Lunn developed a fine system which raised nearly £140 and had a beneficial effect on the fielding. "There is a 50p fine for any slight little thing, misfield, dropped catch, duck, being an idiot or even poor sledging."

The true test of Rick Lunn's ability as a captain will come in his second season, when he is able to bowl at full tilt. "It is not allowing it to regress. That is the key. We will aim to finish third or fourth and on a personal note, bowl more and bat better. As a team if we enjoy it, the rest should all fit together."

Richard Gould: Star Man!
Zak Data

Two years ago, Gomersal star batsman Richard Gould raised a few eye-brows when he terminated his seven-year stay at East Bierley to drop a division to Gomersal.

It was a stroke of genius as the 33 year old's experience and batting performances helped Gomersal gain promotion to the First Division at the end of his first season.

Hitting over 1,000 runs in his second season, he stated his initial aim was to make Gomersal into a good Second Division team and then move them back into the First Division, something which they haven't accomplished since 2003.

Currently in a mid-table position, Gomersal have found the jump from Second to First Division a little challenging. Gould explains " I expected it to be tough and it has been tough. You have to graft more for your runs. After playing for five to ten years against the same bowlers, you get used to them and they get used to you. It has been nice to have that change."

Gould continued "It was a tough decision to leave Bierley. It is an unbelievable club but I couldn't give them 100% commitment. I love the club and I still do some coaching there with the juniors."

Gould had three or four offers from other First Division clubs but he said, "My position meant I was likely to miss half a dozen games, which meant it was difficult to commit to the other clubs. As soon as you mention that, it's not what some clubs are wanting. Speaking to Mick, and the people around Gomersal I knew this would be the right move. I wanted a new challenge and I certainly got one." Gomersal offered the freedom to pursue his accountancy studies and at the same time allow him to work in the healthcare industry.

Gould hasn't dismissed the idea of returning to his former club: "You never know, I might end up back there in the future, maybe not as a player but as a coach."

Tom McCreadie: From Bowler to Batter
Ian Hodgson

Whether it's with a bat in his hand, fielding at slip or in the covers, McCreadie is aggressive by nature. Batting at number six certainly allows him to get on with it, leaving him with a very healthy average last year and a career best score of 98 against Rastrick playing for the Second Xl.

In addition, he "likes to annoy umpires." One spat with official Roger Harrison ended up with a two-match ban. Career highlights include his batting average last season along with getting the chance to partner the now Indian Test match batsman, Wasim Jaffer, while playing for Scholes.

McCreadie had no choice playing for Broad Oak, "forced into it" by his dad, who once played for the First XI. He bowled for the U13s at the age of ten, then U15s and finally U17s when they got to the Semi-Finals of the Walker Cup. His last year U17 was as skipper. As well as getting a trial for Yorkshire Schools, McCreadie represented Huddersfield at U18 and U21 level.

He then went to play for Scholes. At Chapelgate he suffered the yips and didn't bowl again. His batting improved greatly; he'd no choice but to work on it. A First Xl player by the age of 18, he has more or less held down his place since then.

Broad Oak and Scholes aren't the only teams that McCreadie has played for. He went Down Under for four months with Steve Crook and John Bishop. Crook was playing for the club as a *pro* at the time, and currently plays for Northamptonshire.

Tom McCreadie describes Broad Oak as having the best youth structure in the League, and proudly boasts about their "great facilities."

Northowram Fields Collection

Promotion and Respect:
Rob Larner, First XI Captain
Matthew Skirving

Rob Larner has spent the majority of his life excelling at cricket. His talent has seen him take the coveted role of first XI captain at Northowram Fields Cricket Club for the last three years. "They've been three years of varying highs and lows. Gaining promotion to the Premier League then getting relegated the next season, only to be reinstated by a league re-structure are the obvious contrasts," Rob explains.

The club have been plying their trade in the Central Yorkshire Cricket League since 2000, three years after the amalgamation of Fields CC & Northowram CC.

2007 went down as an extraordinary year as he explains, "Winning promotion to the Premier League in 2007 is easily the highlight of my captaincy so far, but personally scoring more than 1,000 runs in that season is also an amazing personal high."

Rob doesn't give the side enough credit, however, stating that they won promotion easily. They won 19 of their 24 games and were promoted to the Premier League for the first time in their history. As well as the team's achievements, he also forgets to mention the four centuries and 11 half-centuries he scored, including a massive 148.

Once in the Premier League the team struggled, which is something they will hope to improve in 2010 as they look to stay in the top division: "Last season was like Hull or West Brom getting promoted to the Premier League in football. It is a very high standard in the CYCL Premier League and it's very intense each week; we had more lows than highs, but the highs were very rewarding."

In modest fashion, Rob states that this is not the most important of his achievements: "The overall highlight of my captaincy is gaining the respect of fellow players, senior players and members alike. Overall, I would say it's been successful in creating an atmosphere in which people want to play for me and the club."

Rob seems to have handled that pressure well, thriving on the situation. It can lead to a hectic lifestyle with little time for much else: "I pick the teams every week, which can be chopping and changing until a Friday night. I net every week and obviously play a full game every weekend, and sometimes double weekends, which can take up a lot of time away from the wife, which is the hardest part ... It is fairly hard trying to manage different people and to try and get the best out of them in certain situations in a game. But overall it is very satisfying, rewarding and very enjoyable."

The future is something they all seem to be looking forward to: "Next season with a number of potential new signings we will have a better squad, which has more experience at this standard, and after our first net practice it looks very encouraging."

Ann Greenwood
Matt Skirving

The first month of the year is slowly dragging by. Yet Ann Greenwood is already organising meetings and indoor nets for the players of Northowram Fields Cricket Club. Her love of cricket came:

> ... basically from supporting my son when he started playing relatively late in his life at 13 years old. The fact that cricket is not an aggressive sport, and is suitable for the whole family to enjoy also grabbed my interest. The best thing about cricket is the fact that it's encouraged as a family sport. It's taken very seriously yet with the humour needed in life so that it doesn't matter should you win or lose the game. As Club Welfare Officer I have many duties: keeping up-to-date CRB checks, making sure the club implements the *Safe Hands* protection policy for children and collating all our information so the coaches can contact parents if need be.

She is known as *Mrs Cricket*. "I think the nickname came from the fact I seemed to end up with, or know where, all the telephone numbers, addresses, bin liners and toilet rolls are." She continues:

My hopes for the future are that we can raise the £500,000 necessary to build a new club house for both the Cricket and Football clubs. This will allow us to continue to grow and further encourage a family community. This will go a long way towards fulfilling most of the committee's, players', coaches' and parents' dreams and acknowledge the hard work over the last three years.

Drawing by Sue Brant

The New Clubhouse
Matt Skirving

One of the biggest factors in Northowram Fields Cricket Club finally gaining its full potential will be the development of the new pavilion/ club house. First XI Captain Rob Larner has emphasised the importance of the new club house, as has Second XI skipper Danny Hensby and committee member Bob Horner.

The only thing is, it's not as easy as it sounds. The costs of building such an impressive new building are weighing down the project. £500,000 is needed. Mrs Cricket herself, Ann Greenwood, testifies, "Fund raising fund raising fund raising, it's all we can do at the moment to try and raise the cash."

There are other avenues that the club is currently investigating and there is some light at the end of the tunnel. The amalgamation of Northowram Fields Cricket Club and Northowram Junior Football Club has brought together twice as many people to try and raise the money.

The amalgamation allows the club to try for a Football Association grant. Unfortunately these grants can take a long time to come to fruition as Ann told me, "The junior football have joined forces with us and we are trying the F.A. for a grant. Everything is quiet at the moment regarding replies for grants but they take forever. We have also tried the ECB, but they can only help with a loan which we can't afford to repay at the moment."

Everyone associated with Northowram Fields is hoping that the money can be raised soon. There is some hope. Ann told me that if they could raise half of the money then the project could start in October 2009.

Upper Hopton Collection

Hopton's Tea Ladies are Top Drawer
Samantha Shilton

Often the unsung heroines of amateur sporting clubs, Upper Hopton's junior catering ladies were bestowed one of the greatest honours recently.

Three ladies, Julie Heaton, Tracy Thompson and Alison Dennison were presented with the coveted President's Award at an awards' bash last November. Of the award, Tracy, 43, said, "It was such a shock for us to receive the award. I had no idea we were going to get a mention, and it was a really nice surprise."

But it is not all awards evenings and limelight. Much of their role within the club involves ordinary, everyday things. "We sell pop, crisps, penny sweets, chocolate and we make teas and coffees," explains Julie. "On match nights we'll make some hot food,

**Photograph by
Richard Turner**

21st Century

usually hot dogs or chip sandwiches, and on weekend mornings we put on bacon sandwiches."

Whilst the work is voluntary, at least one of the women is present at every training session and match. Julie, 42, a previous winner of the award, said, "It was really nice to get the recognition ... a real surprise, and nice that all three of us got to share it."

The women also take on responsibility for organising the teas at home games and quietly manage the little jobs that need doing around the clubhouse, such as keeping the kitchen area clean and taking down old sponsorship signs, all the time smiling and having a laugh.

Katie Aldson and Daniel
Samantha Shilton

Daniel is a First XI player at Upper Hopton, soon to marry Katie Aldson. His preparation for a match day is "fairly routine I'd say, and not that different from any other day."

Daniel takes his dogs out for a long walk around 9am: "I'll play a few games with them, bit of fetch, that sort of thing. It sets me up nicely for the day as it gets my pulse rate up and stretches out my muscles."

He then eats a big breakfast and goes to the supermarket: "I'm not that health conscious so I'll have a fry-up on a match day probably, lots of carbohydrates and protein ... always do a big shop on a Saturday, the weekly shop, at *Asda* at Morley near where I live. Get in some nice food for the week, and I'll pick something out to have for lunch just before I set off for the game."

For lunch, Daniel might have a sandwich and a banana. Then, fiancée Katie helps him prepare for the game: "I'll get my whites out, and Katie will normally iron them for me so they're nice and sharp, as I'm not very good at it myself. Then, yeah, I'll get myself in the car and drive to the game."

Daniel drives over from Batley well before start time: "I like to get to the ground for about 1pm to have a chat with the lads, have a catch up and a bit of gossip. And then we'll all go out onto the field and try and play cricket. I enjoy it most when it's nice and sunny so I can get the old shorts on and have a walk around when I'm not playing, get a bit of a tan."

Depending on how long the game lasts, the team will then head over to the *Traveller's Rest* for a couple of drinks: "Sometimes they might put some food on, some chips or something, and we'll have a pint as it's a nice place to sit. Occasionally we'll discuss going somewhere else after the game, but we usually end up there as it's so close."

After finishing his pint, Daniel then heads home to see his missus and his two sons. "It's not terribly exciting I'm afraid, but that's a typical day for me on a match day."

On top of the world: Sutcliffe Memorial Ground
Daniel Stewart

Upper Hopton Cricket club sits on a series of man-made terraces. The clubhouse, framed by mature trees, feels like a tree-house from which players and supporters get a bird's-eye view of the action.

Cutting up the terrace from the pitch to the clubhouse is a slabbed staircase. Below is the flat expanse of green, the stage upon which the players perform. The views are spectacular.

A Cricket Widow
Lee Hughes (Ms)

Come winters end as spring is sneaking quietly back to life
Recurring nightmares plague a cricket player's wife
In deserted households village wide, widows of the grass
Come to terms with loneliness in a season slow to pass
Keepers of the noble game re-congregate in *whites*
English pastime now revived gives loved ones sleepless nights
Troupes migrate to local pubs following every game

With pint in hand they raise a toast and revel in the fame
In the still small hours tumbling home, much the worse for wear
Drunkenly past the pitch of dreams, slur "thanks" in muddled
prayer
One thing only on their mind, rewarding all their dreams
Winning runs and scores of six on sacred parish greens

Into Cyberspace
Samantha Shilton

As Upper Hopton is very much your typical local cricket club, you
might wonder if a website devoted to it is necessary. Everybody seems
to know everybody else, through family connections or friendship
groups, and the club secretary knows most people's telephone numbers
off by heart.

But webmaster Daniel Heaton, 24, insists that there are many advantages in having a fully functional website:

Obviously the club is small and therefore there are only a small
number of people affiliated with the club. But I update the website twice a week now that we are back in the playing season, and
for the juniors in particular it is nice for them to be able to see
their names up on the website; they seem to enjoy that.

It's useful to have all the fixtures and results up on the site, and

I think that more and more people have started to use it. Parents have access to allow them to plan their week's activities, including dropping the kids off at the club for a game. Social events for the juniors such as BBQs are uploaded to the site. It streamlines the whole process really, people can access the information in their own time and it's much easier than having to ring round everyone.

Is the website effective in attracting new members to the club? "Well, that's the ideal situation obviously, and it's great for the club to have this facility in order for that to happen. Without the website, you're relying on word of mouth to get people joining."

The site has had a *complete rebuild* since Heaton took over 18 months ago, to make it more attractive to prospective parents and players: "I started from scratch really, and my main focus was to create a site that was easy for people to use, but that equally was easy for me to update."

Upper Hopton's website is not only aesthetically pleasing thanks to a variety of pictures on the site, but it is easy to navigate and all information is presented in clear, reader-friendly formats.

Married to Cricket

Self-proclaimed Perfectionist: Lorraine Tucker
Zak Data

At local cricket clubs the tea lady is perceived as a middle-aged woman with an inviting smile whose sole job is to serve tea and snacks. At Scholes Cricket Club (N. Kirklees) this is Mrs Lorraine Tucker who has been serving food and drink for the past five years. She had previously worked at Hallmark but the wholesome and family environment of Scholes Cricket Club lured her into her new career. "My role is everything from bar work to catering to organising events," she states. "We have a good team who work together and make sure we all pull our weight. We are busy every night of the week so we have to keep each other motivated and geared up for the challenge."

On a match day, Lorraine begins at 9 am. The first job is to stock up on basic produce. Once she has taken orders from the players, she hands the list to her team of caterers. As they prepare the food, Lorraine attends to the supporters and customers, serving drinks and meals in the bar and restaurant. She is a self-proclaimed perfectionist and always maintains a high standard of cleanliness and customer service. She knows her punters' favourite food, "They absolutely love my hotpots. I make sure I've prepared a lot of them."

She was initially drawn into the club through her children, watching them play cricket for the Scholes junior team. Her son James, 21, recently broke into the First XI and is a talented all-rounder. Her younger boys are also keen footballers. Outside cricket Lorraine reads novels and has recently became a grandmother.

Julie Walker
Richard Crouch

How did you become involved at Hopton Mills Cricket Club?

Initially I became involved at the club because my husband played at the club and I used to go down and watch him play. When I was there I started asking questions about why certain things were not being done and why some men were not taking more of a role in traditional female roles at the club, such as making the teas. From there I started to become involved in the club.

What is your current role at Hopton Mills Cricket Club?

I am currently the Chairperson at the club and I undertake all sorts of different jobs. I see to the general running of the club, I chair committee meetings and I order everything the club needs for the bar and teas. I also do the teas at the games on a weekend.

How do the male members of the club treat you?

It was very difficult at first. The male members did not really take to me holding the role of Chairperson at the club; there was a bit of hostility. The officials from the League really did not take to me at first. When I became Chairperson, women were not invited to the League dinners at the end of the season, so I began to ask why women were not invited. Women are now invited to the League dinners so I would say men have come round to the idea of women playing a more significant role in cricket.

Are there any other roles that women play at Hopton Mills?

Yes, there are quite a number of ladies involved at the club. The Treasurer is female and it is a lady that takes care of IT, posters and the writing of the club minutes. I would say the committee is more or less made up of equal numbers of men and women. Women are not just responsible for the teas anymore; they carry out more significant roles in the club.

Do you think women have become more interested in cricket?

Yes, I think female interest in cricket has increased at Hopton Mills from when I first became involved at the club. There are more and more girls coming down and actually playing cricket which is a very positive thing and we are trying to encourage female coaches as well. With the junior section as well we get a lot of interest from the mothers of the players; they give a lot of support and help out quite a lot at the club.

Is it more acceptable for women to become involved in cricket?

Yes, I think it has become more acceptable in recent years but there is still a long way to go yet; we are on a long road but it is gradually getting better for women to become involved. To begin with, women were pretty much ignored in most aspects of the cricket club but it is getting better now and women are playing much more of a role at the club both on the field with girls teams and also behind the scenes with me as the Chairperson.

Emley Collection

Thewayforward.co.uk: The Emley Website
Chris Knowles

In the current age of new technology and on-demand media, the Internet offers unlimited possibilities for suppliers of content and audiences from many walks of life. Take, for instance, the Emley Clarence website.

The website allows club information to be viewed by an unlimited number of people. News items are displayed alongside upcoming events and fund raisers, in addition to player stats and club results. Layout is straightforward yet effective, displaying the necessary information on the home page and with clear links to other pages on the site, all presented in the club's colours. The site advertises Emley's sponsors throughout.

Credit has to be given to Ros Moors, the webmaster, who works very hard to maintain the site.

Emley's Clubmark
Chris Knowles

The information evening held at the *Wentworth* Pub one night in 2007/8 highlighted the key areas of Emley's proposal for Clubmark status, a national accreditation which rewards sports clubs with successful junior organisation and leadership.

Once acquired, an array of funding sources becomes available. In the case of Emley Clarence, the financial support will contribute to a new clubhouse which has been designed and permission for building obtained. The funding sources include the National Lottery, Sport England (a public body working closely with the Government to distribute sporting funds), banks and even local councils.

There are several areas on which *Clarence* will be assessed. First, duty of care and safeguarding children is covered by the quality of registers taken at training sessions, the "in case of an accident" procedure and the amount of emergency numbers the coaches must have in their possession. Second, the programme of cricket on offer and the level of coaching that is available which will facilitate the progression of children through the age groups and into the Second XI. Other assessments include whether or not *Clarence* is operating on an equal opportunities-basis and the extent of parents' involvement.

Jeanette Stratford
Chris Knowles

"I used to watch Craig play and obviously ferry him around as was necessary!" Jeanette explains. "You find yourself gradually getting much more involved and drawn into the set-up. I'm on the committee now and have been for three years or so and I'm also involved with the fund raising committee."

Jeanette is loosely involved in the junior set-up with Child Welfare Officer, Sue Tedder. "I'm meant to be her assistant actually! We're supposed to be going on a course to be accredited in that line of work but they're few and far between and we haven't been available to take it yet."

Clubmark is an extremely important accreditation, paving the way for future sponsorship and funding. There is an awful lot of paperwork and the whole process takes a great deal of time.

Last year, Jeanette was voted Emley's Club Person of the Year. She admitted, "It was a total shock really! I just go about my committee job, getting involved and helping where I can, so it was very nice to be recognised for that." She continued:

I know my children have had hours of pleasure thanks to this club and you've got to put something back in so that the club can progress forward. I hope we can maintain what we've achieved so far. This season may prove to be more difficult with fund raising and we need to get on with it early to make the most of it. Everyone at the club is wholeheartedly involved and wants to see the club doing well. I really hope the first team stay up and I would love to see the seconds get promoted; obviously after what happened last year that would be great.

Sue Tedder
Chris Knowles

How did you first become involved with Emley Clarence?

Initially, I would take my children to their junior matches and, at first, I was just another parent really. I always watched the matches and we also did refreshments so I began getting more and more involved in that way.

What made you decide to offer more of your time?

Jeanette and I are good friends and we wanted to have a say in the running of the club. We thought the men didn't always get it right and we thought we could offer something to the committee.

How did the Child Welfare Officer at Emley come about?

I work at a school and so child protection is something which I have had experience of in the past. But it's silly really, I have to have yet another qualification for the juniors at the cricket club and you find that whatever you do it's a separate application each time.

How were you introduced to the Clubmark scheme?

I first heard about Clubmark at my school and had some details sent through because I thought it should be something that Emley should be doing. In order for the club to become bigger and better, and attract more funding, you need to base a lot of what you are doing around young people.

How will that contribute to the junior set-up at the club?

It really does help with sponsorship and companies are more willing to help if you're seen to be doing the right thing which is giving good quality training to young people. Parents are aware that, like a lot of things, money is important and they are willing to pay for the best for their children. It's our duty to offer this quality service through the junior set-up or we can't expect them to come back.

When will the application be ready to submit?

I hope to have the Clubmark application ready by the end of the year. It's a lot of work organising the paperwork and I have to fit it around everything else, of course, but we need to have a look how far off we are first.

How many children do you anticipate signing on this season?

Last year we signed on around 50 children of different age groups and we're hoping that we can do the same this year. We'd welcome as many as possible, of course, because, eventually, a healthy junior section makes for a healthy club.

Simon Lewis
Chris Knowles

Simon Lewis joined Emley Clarence when he was 16 years old having been part of the junior set-up at local rivals Kirkburton CC.

Originally a bowler, Simon exchanged ball for bat some time ago and is currently used as a relief bowler if necessary. The 30 year old became a Second XI player at the age of 17 and quickly showed the promise which earned him promotion to the First XI soon after.

Simon was an integral part of the First XI team that won both the Central League title and the Allsop Cup in 2000 and he tells me, "That was one of my finest achievements. I was opening bat for that season and it was a great success to do the double, especially when you're involved in the team." He continues, "Another great moment for me was hitting my maiden century in 2003 for the First Team."

Having returned to the Second XI in the last couple of years due to commitments at work, Simon enjoyed huge success last season, picking up the Player of the Year award. The award is voted by fellow Second team players and is enormous recognition. Simon explains, "It was a tight run thing because no-one really stood out. Everyone contributed last season and I'd say all the players won us a game individually at some point. We all thought it could have been a close one last year, though."

Simon is rarely off the field of play as he is currently one of the club's groundsmen, having succeeded Cliff Smith, who had previously held the post for eight years. Simon explains, "I'd say I've been groundsman for three seasons now, with the exception of six months. I had various work commitments and so I found it hard at one stage to find the necessary time. I just like the idea of it. I work with Ken Taylor, a First XI player, and between us we share the duties throughout the season."

Simon is no longer Treasurer. He says, "I chose not to be because of the amount of time the role of groundsman takes up on its own." It did have its advantages though, as he tells me, "It was very demanding but you didn't have to go to anyone else regarding money for the ground, because I was the Treasurer!"

And on his present role, Simon admits, "It's a full-time job: cutting, maintaining, or just trying to get rid of something! We had moles this winter and we had some trouble getting rid of them up until recently. I think they're gone now!"

Miscellany

Umpires
David Brenchley

It can be said that sportsmen take officials for granted. Football authorities have only recently started taking action to stamp out bad behaviour whereas, historically, cricketers have always respected their umpires.

Now, with the invention of devices like *Hawkeye*, umpires' decisions are being questioned more often. Even without these technologies, Andrew Wray feels that umpires are given a tough time: "People are very competitive these days and they are taught to question. You know that the batter's hit it and you're fairly certain the batter knows he has hit it but until you put your finger up, he won't go."

Wray, who finished playing cricket for Outlane at the age of 48, has been umpiring for 20 years. He has taken charge of two Sykes Cup Finals, with eight years between. "They are big days; at a normal League match on a Saturday or Sunday you get 40 to 100 people, occasionally 200. At a Sykes Cup Final you get 700 to 1000 people paying to get in and everybody wants to win."

Wray remembers his first Final between Elland and Scholes: "Elland won comfortably; it wasn't a nail-biter but the Elland professional took seven wickets and won the Man of the Match award." The second match he umpired was in 2006, when underdogs Barkisland overcame Delph and Dobcross.

Wray found umpiring was not as easy as it seemed: "It's a long learning curve because you don't know the rules. You think you do but you don't. It's a game where you have to say no to people and that's never easy because some people don't like it. I still go to refresher courses. I go to one every year but I subsequently got my ACU badge (Association of Cricket Umpires) which, in theory, enables you to umpire anywhere." Although he hasn't officiated at county level, Wray has taken charge of a few matches involving Yorkshire's Second XI.

Wray prefers to know the players, "They all have idiosyncrasies; you get bowlers who never bowl a no-ball and you get others who are a nightmare. You're watching their front feet and they are constantly no-balling."

Does he have any advice for any prospective umpires? "If you're going to be any good at umpiring you very quickly learn, 'to thine own self be true.' I have often said to the bowler 'if I think he is out I will give him out.' You mustn't level up [if you make a mistake], you can't just think oh, I'll give the next fella out, you have to live with it."

The BOLA Cricket Bowling Machine
Mark Edmonds

Barkisland Cricket Club has recently enlisted the help of possibly the world's greatest bowler as the club prepares itself for the 2008 season. Although not the talkative type, the bowler can reach speeds of up to 100 miles per hour, whilst being able to swing the ball both ways with unerring accuracy. If that wasn't enough, the seven and a half footer is also as adept a spinner as you could ever wish to see, with the ability to bowl both off-spin and leg-spin. Unfortunately, this bowler cannot bat or field, nor are they eligible to represent the side on match days.

The BOLA Cricket Bowling Machine is housed at Huddersfield New College but could prove crucial in the club's pre-season preparations. With bowlers unable to reach full speed due to the shortened indoor run-up, batsmen are not able to hone their timing of the fastest balls in time for the start of the season. The BOLA machine is the best available training resource for cricketers, with every county side in possession of at least one of them.

Players typically use the machine as a pair for a period of 15 minutes. This involves a batsman at each end with the on-strike batsman facing

an over from the machine. After the sixth ball, the two players run three, leaving the previously off-strike player on-strike. This process then continues for the session, irrespective of being bowled out.

"What this does is increase the heart-rate of the players and gives them a rush of adrenaline" says the College's cricket coach Dave Weston. "Running three makes them both physically and mentally tired, meaning that they're not at 100 per cent when they face a delivery." The reasoning, concludes Dave: "the running between the wicket helps to create a match situation rather than standing in the nets and being totally focused."

Players between the ages of 16 and 18 are coming from Leeds and Bradford to the College to use this equipment as part of four sessions they undertake each week. "It's only going to improve the youngsters" Dave enthuses. "They're going to be able to face quality bowling throughout the year, instead of just the summer months. Who knows, some of them might even end up at Barkisland!"

"It's great for everyone that faces it," says Chairman Steve Casaru, feeding the balls into the machine. "It gives us the chance to really work on a player's technique by being able to put the ball right where we want it, every time we want it to." Another ball thuds in the batter's front pad. "He's got to learn to get that leg out the way!"

Lahore Horror
Zak Data

In March of this year, a gang of heavily armed gunmen ambushed Sri Lanka's national cricket team, killing six police guards and wounding seven players. The Sri Lankans were travelling to the city's Gaddafi Stadium for the third day of the second Test Match against Pakistan at around 9 am local time.

The players reported injured were Thilan Samaraweera, Kumar Sangakkara, Ajantha Mendis, Mahela Jayawardene, Tharanga Paranavithana and Chaminda Vaas. Two of them were admitted to hospital.

What fans of local cricket may not be aware of is that former Hanging Heaton star Thilan Thushara was part of the Sri Lankan team. Thilan, 28, father of one, was playing in his fourth Test Match. Whilst Thushara's legs were cut by flying shrapnel he has not suffered any long-term damage.

Hanging Heaton Cricket Club secretary Nat Lawrence described Thushara as down-to-earth and quiet. His record at Hanging Heaton was impeccable.

Lawrence said "Everyone at Hanging Heaton was shocked. I was very close to Thushara when he played for us and I always keep track on his international career. I was aware he was on the bus but not that he was injured. We have mutual friends so I spoke to them directly to make sure he was fine."

Pakistan, India, Sri Lanka and Bangladesh are due to jointly host the cricket World Cup in 2011. The attacks in Pakistan are expected to have huge consequences for the cricket world, with the ICC considering whether Pakistan can co-host the World Cup.

Dad's Matches (My son the cricketer part II)
David Walker

When my son Chris was cricket daft, I was the transport and took him everywhere. He attended a private school. It didn't make a difference to his local pals, or if it did, I never spotted it. His First XI cricket team photo is still a proud possession. It didn't matter that they only had one team and a bit of a ragbag at that. The boys enjoyed it hugely and put up with the jibes from the opposition for being stuck up. We played at Royds Hall and Salendine Nook Schools on very dubious tracks and one evening down at Paddock next to the railway cutting. The most notable thing that night, in addition to the cricket, was the master who umpired. A Doctor in Physics teaching geography. He gave one of the lads out lbw from square leg. *Plonker.*

Chris's first headmistress was a *Barbie Doll*. She left in a hurry after her husband got in a little over his head trying to buy Manchester United. She was replaced by two sensible experienced ladies who we met with the rest of the staff every year at parents' evening. There was also a lovely French teacher who took them abroad and threatened to tuck them in every night with a kiss.

And I played in the dads' cricket match. In front of a pleasing two storey double fronted stone building, apparently donated by a Huddersfield worthy - a Crowther, or a Ramsden maybe. Some of the dads took it seriously and wore whites. I wore a livid blue tracksuit which the sports master found amusing. Chris had two overs at me, but I coped. I batted left-handed with a bloke who took his jacket off and played in collar, tie and braces. He owned an electrical shop in town.

We also had a dad's match at the local cricket club; an altogether more serious affair which nearly ended in a brawl. I don't think they've arranged another one. Flyn umpired. I skippered. The boys had had a good run in the cup and the dads all knew each other pretty well. Just one real cricketer who played for Cartworth Moor and sold expensive blinds. His son was barely taller than a full-size bat. Used to wear his kit in the front room and practice his shots, so his dad said. He was really a tennis player and went to clinics in Spain. I did say they were expensive blinds! The other dads weren't cricketers, but they were keen as mustard to win.

The boys batted first. We'd two overs apiece, a question of getting it on the wickets and hoping. I fielded at short mid off and started the aggravation by taking a catch. It wasn't that I caught it, but the way I caught it. I was minding my own business, seemingly not taking a lot of notice. One of the lads played a bit early and lofted one at arms length above my left shoulder. My arm shot out and plucked the ball out of the air. Bit like a frog catching a fly with its tongue. Then I nonchalantly tossed the ball over my shoulder and walked away. No one moved for a couple of seconds. There were a couple of expletives and mutterings from the pavilion, but the lad had to go.

When we batted the chap from Cartworth Moor got us close and it was all about whether the non-cricketing dads could get bat on ball. The boys were excited by every wicket they took and cross at a good shot or misfield. We coached from the boundary edge, "Hit it here." "There's a run there." "Two, keep running." The closer we got the louder it all became. Three to win off the final over and the ground was bedlam. One of the dads got a streaky four and that was it. Uproar. Tears and protests on one side, smiles and backslaps on the other. The boys wouldn't speak to us. I think we overdid it a bit.

I didn't dare look at Flyn. I just knew that tired smile would be there. The tutting and the shaking of the head would follow soon.

Rocky and Local Rules: Sunday 15 January, Appletreewick v Malhamdale
Tony Hutton

Less than three weeks since our last cricket match of 2005 (the traditional Boxing Day game between North Leeds and the Northern Cricket Society) a party of five were in a large field opposite the *New Inn* in the Dales village of Appletreewick, well before the scheduled start.

We had just established when the game would be played when the Malhamdale team and supporters came marching down the middle of the road from the nearby *Craven Arms*. We followed them into the New Inn, where it soon became apparent that most of them had other priorities than cricket. As I patiently waited my turn at the crowded bar, the tone was set by the man in front of me ordering 14 pints of bitter. So we had a drink and some lunch, by which time it was almost 2.30 pm and getting both darker and colder. With some reluctance, the players took the field about 2.45pm with the number of overs reduced from 20 to 10 a side.

The players were dressed in a variety of winter clothing, but at least the umpires wore white coats. One of them had a bottle of whisky in his pocket, the other a bottle of wine. These were not solely to keep the umpires warm, but were for the benefit of the players as well. One of the many local rules seemed to be that each bowler had a swig from a bottle before the start of each over. Other rules seemed to be no lbws, you could not be out first ball, and you could not hit a boundary first ball, so a big hit had to be all run. It was far too complicated for us non-locals, so we just went with the flow and joined in when the whisky bottle was passed round the spectators.

A major talking-point was the appearance of a man for Malhamdale with county experience. He was Paul *Rocky* Ridgeway who had been on the Lancashire staff and who we had seen opening the bowling for Lancashire Second XI. When his turn came to bowl he set nine slips and took a very long run, only to serve up a series of donkey drops. His contribution to the game did not seem to have much effect on the result.

After an exciting last ball finish, the two scorers, one of them armed with a hot water bottle, declared the result a tie on 81-5 each. Our own perusal of the scorebook suggested that Malhamdale had won by three runs. But nobody cared and all 70 people present, players and spectators included, retired to the pub for the more serious part of proceedings.

Some months later we found an enjoyable report of the game on the Malhamdale website. Unfortunately, it contained one major error: "The crowd was amazingly swelled by a group of Lancashire cricket enthusiasts, who had traced this annual event on the Malhamdale website and came to spectate." As four of us are residents of Yorkshire (although one was born in Lincolnshire), and only one from Lancashire, we took great exception to this and at the time of writing are still waiting for an official apology.

Interlude - III
The Final that Took Weeks and Weekes
Up Against It
Allan Stuttard

The Wood Cup committee, in their wisdom, decided that Werneth in Oldham would be drier, but surprise surprise, it rained again.

The match finally started on 12 August when Middleton scored 24 for 0. By 16 August they were 96 for 2, reaching 150 for 4 on August 23 when, under Cup rules, the innings was suspended.

On Thursday 26 August Walsden commenced their innings without Weekes who had a long standing commitment in Ireland. It's not clear what that commitment was, maybe cricket, maybe golf, but it seems, according to *Walsden Cricket and Bowling Club Newsletter*, he became stranded on the wrong side of the Irish Sea. Without him, Walsden slumped to 45 for 5, at which point Jimmy Wilkinson was 10 not out. Weekes finally arrived at the crease on 27 August with his side on 46 for 6. He told Jim to count the deliveries in each 8-ball over. "We'll run on the last one," he said. At close of play Walsden were 132 for 6. Weekes had scored 83 out of the 87 runs added. The following night, when the 100 partnership had been reached to great applause, Jim miscounted and had to face 3 balls. He blocked two and then cracked the final half volley through the covers, whereupon Weekes ran down the wicket, "Don't try and win this bloody match on your own!"

Drawing by Clive Hetherington

5 - Timeless

Holmbridge

Beginnings, Survival and Growth

Mytholmroyd Methodists: 1894 to present day
Stuart Greenwood

The club was established in 1894 as Mytholmroyd Wesleyan Sunday School Cricket Club. Most of the membership/fixture cards from 1894 to the present have survived.

The club kept a close relationship with the church, always holding meetings and AGMs at the Sunday School. In 1894, the Sunday School had many scholars and teachers old enough to make up two teams. All players had to attend services a minimum number of times on Sundays in order to play. Until the 1970s, the Minister at the Church was automatically the President.

The officials of the club in 1894 included Walker Waddington (54 years a Sunday School teacher), J Moore, JE Helliwell, T Sager and several Greenwoods.

Opponents in the first year included Cragg Vale United, Booth, Salem, Lumbutts, Todmorden Church, Norland, Roomfield Baptists and Elland Wesleyans. It seems that most cricket clubs in this area were based on churches, of several denominations. Many also had tennis and football teams.

The club finally settled at The Holmes ground on Scout Road in 1906. Before this they had been at Bent (1894), Redacre (1896), The Holmes (nearer to Cragg Road 1897-1901), Bent again and Banksfields (1904-05).

The club played in the Calder Valley League for 11 years before joining the newly formed Hebden Bridge League in 1906. In the 1940s they were in the Halifax Amateur League and in 1952 joined the Halifax

League, winning their first match against the mighty Greetland!

During the war years the club, despite having only one team, still kept up fixtures. The church has a large framed photograph of 11 members of the club who lost their lives in the 1914-1918 War. This is a sober reminder of the impact the war had on the club, the church and the community.

We have collected a number of photographs, newspaper cuttings and scorebooks. Some of the rules were as follows:

That any member using improper language or indulging in any questionable conduct shall be reported to the Committee and dealt with by the same.

In practice, no bowler shall keep on bowling for more than 10 minutes after another member has asked for the ball.

That during practice, no person shall bat more than 5 minutes per innings.

All new members' names shall be submitted to the Selection Committee for approval before being accepted as a member.

Members shall conduct themselves as gentlemen affiliated to the Scout Road Methodist Church and Sunday School, both as regards the actual game, and also in the spirit of cricket from day to day.

Prior to practice, the pitch shall be cut, rolled and measured to the correct length.

Over the years the facilities at the ground have changed, slowly some would say and not by much. The old pavilion which was there after the Second World War had the scorers placed high up a vertical ladder with a great view. This was replaced possibly in the late 1940s. A flagpole was added and a green and yellow flag (club colours also sported on club caps) flown on match days. In the 1950s the score hut was the old tea hut now sited over by Scout Road car park. Alongside there was a *new* tea hut made from an old chicken hut, I think, plus a covered seating area for about five people!

In about 1963 the present pavilion was erected. It was the Primary Department Room at Mount Zion Primitive Methodist Church in

Mytholmroyd and was brought over when the two village Methodist churches joined together.

The present Canteen was originally the tennis pavilion at Nutclough, Hebden Bridge and was brought down in sections by lorry. It replaced a smaller one on the same site which earlier had been the office of Crossleys *Nuts and Bolts*, Cragg Road.

Up until the 1960s, water was collected from the well in the top corner of the field or from Mrs Sutcliffe's house in Scout Road. Running water (cold) came into the canteen first, then much later into the changing rooms. Hot water is still obtained from a modern gas boiler. Electricity has been discussed but that's all. A flush toilet arrived ready for the 21stCentury.

Cricket and Churches
Peter Davies

Almondbury Wesleyans, Mirfield Parish Cavaliers, and Crossbank Methodists are three existing cricket clubs in Kirklees who advertise their historic religious affiliation in their name. Go back a few decades and every village boasted one or more teams with church connections: Honley Wesleyans, Ravensthorpe Congregationals, Almondbury Zion, Birchencliffe Church, Salendine Nook Baptists, Emley Nonconform-

ists, Hanging Heaton Parish Church. There were also leagues dedicated exclusively to church-based teams such as the Batley & Dewsbury Sunday School League.

What explains this trend? In the nineteenth century, it was common for religious bodies of most denominations to provide recreational opportunities for their congregations. This is often viewed as churches showing a resolve to improve the health of the body as well as of the mind, via rational recreation; part of a general movement to re-form traditional working-class leisure habits. Promoting these activities was also an effective means of encouraging church attendance.

Paddock, Spen Victoria and Mirfield based Moorlands all had Methodist origins. The Spen club evolved out of Cleckheaton Wesleyan Sunday School, while Moorlands were connected to Dewsbury Moorlands Methodist Church. Early Moorlands players had to sign a register every time they attended Sunday School or church so as to determine eligibility for the cricket team.

Heckmondwike & Carlinghow CC emerged out of Upper Chapel, a magnificent congregational church. Reports on the infant Upper Chapel CC appeared in every edition of the church manual. The club became Heckmondwike URC CC and then Heckmondwike & Carlinghow United CC.

The Church of England encouraged the growth of many clubs. Slaithwaite was known as Slaithwaite St. James's CC in its early years, while the embryonic Golcar St. Johns CC used to hold meetings in the church school. In 1881 the Vicar of Gomersal, the Rev RF Taylor, founded Gomersal St Mary's CC, while at Emley the rector between 1886 and 1900, the Rev E Sutton, used to sit in the centre of the front row in team photographs. In the early Twentieth Century, however, Broad Oak had to be very diplomatic with the Vicar of Christ Church, Linthwaite, who at one point wanted to evict them from their ground!

The location of cricket grounds may indicate a historic link between clubs and churches. The headquarters of Broad Oak and Heckmondwike & Carlinghow United are a mere six-hit away from the churches they had connections with. Golcar and Almondbury Wesleyans are located only half a mile from St. John's Parish and Almondbury Methodists.

And that still leaves traditional village clubs like Kirkburton, Thurstonland, and Holmbridge, who, literally, play in the shadow of churches, even though they have no historic connection with them. Up until the 1970s Holmbridge could not play after 6pm on a Sunday, such was the bond that existed between their mill-owner landlord and nearby St. David's Parish Church. In fact, as soon as the church bells rang for Sunday evensong, players and umpires had to adjourn the game till Monday night!

Some clubs threw off their church links, like Honley St. Mary's in 1879. They disconnected themselves from the local parish church "to improve the efficiency of the club … and that the club should be open to anyone subject to the approval of the committee."

Conversely, clubs like Crossbank Methodists, from the Batley-Birstall area, recently voted to keep their religious affiliation, even though Crossbank Methodist Church has long been demolished. They chose to keep "Methodists" in their name because, perceptively, club members realised that the church connection was part of their proud heritage.

What is also interesting is that some clubs without church links have actually forged a relationship. After a pavilion fire in 2002, Dewsbury based Westborough CC had nowhere to serve sandwiches and cakes during the tea interval. So they approached their local chapel, Westborough Methodist, and an agreement was struck to mutual advantage.

And finally, full marks to the Vicar of Thurstonland, the Rev. Jerome, who in the first decade of the Twentieth Century, regularly gave his local club "assistance with a wheelbarrow to move the large mounds of earth" when members were working on the ground.

Down the Generations

The Family Moss
Allan Stuttard

I have been fortunate in my career (if that is the correct description) to play in the same league as Frank Tyson, Chester Watson and Roy Gilchrist. Gilchrist was certainly fast and, when he threw the ball, he was bloody fast. So a pinch of salt comes to mind when fast-bowling claims are made.

When I read in a centenary handbook of the Ribblesdale League that

Sam Moss of Padiham was the fastest bowler in England, I just had to look into it further. Could he be the grandfather of Roger who was my best man? Sure enough, in Roger's attic, there was the ball that took 10 wickets, all clean bowled, against Great Harwood on 15 August 1908. Next to it was the stump he broke during the following week's fixture with Barrow.

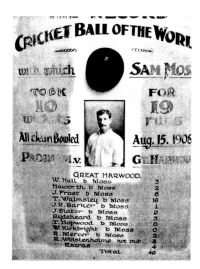

Sam Moss began his career at Merthyr Tydfil in 1891. He took 100 wickets both there and at his next club, the Plymouth Works team. He then moved to the Manchester Cricket Club, Old Trafford, where he took 90 wickets at 10 runs apiece and was said to be faster than Arthur Mould. He was selected for the Lancashire Second Eleven, but, against Surrey at The Oval, he was called for throwing. He didn't play for the county again.

The teams he subsequently played for make a long list: Newcastle-on-Tyne (1895); Haslingden in the Lancashire League (1896); Bacup (1898) where he took 143 wickets at 8.2 before being banned again for throwing; Burslem and Walsall in the Staffordshire League. Whilst in the Midlands, he took 6 for 62 representing Staffordshire against the South of England and 337 wickets at 4 apiece in three years with Walsall. The list continues: 103 wickets for Batley in 1905; deputised for Barnsley against Huddersfield (took all 10 wickets); Padiham in 1908 and 1909; after the war, in which he served as a Second Lieutenant in the Air Force, he played in the Yorkshire leagues.

He was fatally struck by a train on his way to a match. *Wisden*, in 1924, wrote:

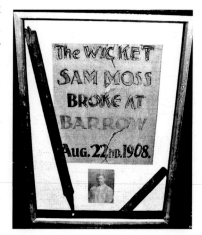

Moss, Sam, reputed to have been at one time the fastest bowler in England, was killed on the railway line whilst walking to a match at Featherstone on August 7 (1923).

He must have been a remarkably fast bowler. Mr Milford wrote in the *Bacup Times*:

Moss had been bowling for two hours when I played forward to him. The ball popped up a little and struck the shoulder of my bat. Off any other bowler I should expect to be caught at slip, but off Sam I was caught at gully on the boundary edge over 100 yards away.

But the story does not end yet. Sam's son, Ernest, became a journey-man professional cricketer for Birstall in 1912, moving to Featherstone for the three years prior to the war. On demobilisation he joined Tong Park followed by Batley where he stayed for four seasons. He created a Yorkshire Council record in 1921; 124 wickets at 7.5. In 1923, the year of his father's death, he was selected by Glamorgan, his county of birth, against Lancashire at Blackpool. He then crossed over to the Lancashire League with Todmorden (1924-25), where he started a shoe repair business, and Ramsbottom (1926). In 1934 he cut his thumb and died two weeks later, aged 40, of blood poisoning.

One Saturday when Ernest was playing at Todmorden, a carnival passed by. Not unnaturally it competed for the crowd's attention and many spectators left the ground. Whilst they were away Ernest took a hat trick which hardly anyone witnessed.

Ernest had three sons with a reputation to uphold. My friend Roger was no more than a good Second XI player with Walsden. Older broth-er Len, however, became a renowned amateur with Walsden and Tod-morden, playing 25 years in the Central Lancashire League. It's said he would have progressed further but for the Second World War. He also played professional football with Burnley and non-league Mossley.

One story about Len concerns a game against Milnrow who had Dusty Rhodes as professional. It was Wakes Week and Len had a bus to catch to Blackpool. He set about Rhodes' bowling and scored 50 in no time. When Dusty came off the field for a moment, someone overheard him: "I have played all over the world and I have never been hit like that before. I am not going back on until Moss has gone and caught his bus."

So who was the fastest? I've got the salt pot ready!

120 Not Out! The Moorhouse Family
Paul Rai

During the 1880s a man named George Moorhouse pulled on the Armitage Bridge whites for the first time. Over 120 years later, his family is still an important part of the club.

George and brother Robert were integral parts of the great 1887 Lumb Cup triumph, Robert making three scores of over 50 en route to the Final. Robert, known as Bob, made his first-class debut for Yorkshire in 1888 against Cambridge University, scoring 42 before being clean bowled. He was dismissed for a duck in the second innings.

Bob played 217 first-class matches for Yorkshire, scoring over 5,000 runs and taking 49 wickets. On retiring, he played as professional at a number of clubs and was a coach at Sedbergh public school.

A third Moorhouse brother, Fred, moved away to play first-class cricket for Warwickshire, aged 20. He stood over six feet and, as a fast bowler, would have been able to extract steep bounce. He took 260 first-class wickets in 117 matches at an average of 23.96. These figures included five wickets in an innings on eight occasions and ten wickets in a match two times. His best performance was 7 for 53.

Abraham Moorhouse appeared for Armitage Bridge between 1900 and 1930. Known as Abe, he won the league fielding prize in 1924. During World War Two, he came out of retirement to captain the Second XI. He retired again in the early fifties when he was struck in the face by the ball. He has been committee member, Secretary and league representative.

Abe's son Roy began life as Second XI scorer in 1942. Mostly a Second XI player, he was in the 1953 Paddock Shield runners-up side and was appointed Captain for a number of seasons. Like his father, he joined the committee, became Secretary and for a brief spell was Club Chairman. To cap off a great career, Roy was awarded the Lady Sykes Trophy in 1973.

Into the 1980s and Roy's son, Robert, was part of the Second XI who won two Paddock Shields and three championship titles, two as Captain. In 1983 he won the League Second XI bowling prize.

Robert's sons, James and Danny, have represented Armitage Bridge. Danny broke into the first team last year, scoring his first 50 at the age of 17. He bowled 81 overs: 13 maidens, 14 wickets for 377 runs at an average of 26.93. He was also part of the U17 side that won its section and reached the Walker Cup Final.

Nine Moorhouses - George, Bob, Fred, Abe, Harry (Abe's brother), Roy, Robert, James and Danny - have played for Armitage Bridge Cricket Club over the last 120 years.

(Armitage Bridge CC was established in 1839 and plays in the Huddersfield League)

Professionals

Sylvester Oliver
Brian Heywood

The professionals' board at Todmorden contains the following inscription:

To the Memory of Sylvester Oliver: Professional and Friend

Syl signed as Todmorden's professional in 1959, a young West Indian far from his home state of Trinidad. A natural and talented all-rounder, Syl had been twelfth man for the West Indies in 1958, the closest he came to playing in an international. The West Indies team was very strong at this time and it was tough to get selected.

Syl's fielding was electrifying, athletic in the outfield and brilliant close to the bat. He batted with style and aggression and bowled with pace and hostility.

In 1960, Todmorden slipped from third to sixth in the League and he was not re-signed for 1961. Syl signed for Marsden in the Huddersfield League where he performed so well that Todmorden re-signed him in 1964. Returning to the club, he was clearly more mature. He had cut down his pace and learned to use English conditions to his advantage, swinging the ball in the air and gaining deviation off the pitch. His batting was more consistent and Todmorden happily extended his stay as professional to five seasons, bringing his total to seven which remains the most by one professional at the club since the 1850s.

In 1965, a shoulder injury sustained whilst away *sub-proing* in Huddersfield blighted Syl's season and he was never able to throw powerfully again. Syl took 114 wickets and a club record 26 catches in 1966 as the team finished third in the League and runners-up in the Worsley Cup. In his last two seasons he held together a weakening team. In Syl's seven seasons the team never finished lower than sixth out of the 14 clubs; in the first two seasons after he left Todmorden, they finished in the bottom three.

In total for Todmorden, Syl scored 3942 runs, including 31 fifties, and took 504 wickets, including five or more wickets in an innings on 46 occasions.

Syl was also professional at Walsden in the Central Lancashire League, Egerton in the Bolton League, Almondbury in the Huddersfield League, Winnington Park in the Cheshire County League and Newton Heath in the Manchester Association. All these clubs have Syl stories to tell. A favourite memory of many teammates is Syl's careful planning but unclear communication when positioning his fielders "Not on that piece of grass there, on that piece of grass there!"

Syl returned to Todmorden as coach in the 1980s. He went on the club's pre-season tour to Bristol in 1981 and was never happier than when invited back to play in a charity, benefit or friendly match. He played for the Lancashire over-50s team, still a formidable cricketer. In a friendly match at Todmorden in 1990 he took a brilliant catch close to the bat and, whilst everyone was scanning the boundary trying to see where the ball had gone, Syl had it in his pocket!

Timeless

In 1999, still enjoying excellent health, Syl went on holiday to his native Trinidad. He picked up a virus and died suddenly. A memorial service held in Todmorden was attended by representatives of all his league clubs. There was standing room only in St Mary's Church.

Crossing the Pennines, Stuart Fletcher
Ian Hirst

There are some conventions in sport. In football, for example, never return to a club that you have managed and had success with, like Kevin Keegan. Or, never play for a rival club, unless if you are Denis Law, who played for both the red and the blue halves of Manchester.

It's the same with cricket. It is difficult to play for both the White Rose county and the Red Rose county. Yet Stuart Fletcher did.

Born in 1964 in Keighley, Fletcher made his county debut in 1983 against Middlesex at Headingley. During his time in county cricket Fletcher took 240 wickets in 114 matches, which included five five-wicket hauls with best figures of 8 for 58 in 1988 for Yorkshire against Essex. He also had an impressive economy rate of 3.31 and an average of 34.89. On the one-day circuit he played 132 matches, taking 166 wickets with best figures of 4 for 11.

Fletcher was a member of the Yorkshire side which won the Benson and Hedges Trophy in 1987 when he took 2 for 37 against a strong Northamptonshire side.

He made the controversial move to Lancashire in 1992 without success and went on to play in the Minor Counties with Lincolnshire. He later returned to club cricket with Woodlands at Oakenshaw in the Bradford League and in 2001 stepped over to the Huddersfield League.

Fletcher settled at Elland where his services continue to be called upon, though he's hoping, once the youngsters come through, he will not be needed as much in the future. This season he took over from Dennis Midwood as Chairman.

His son, Craig, is building on the Fletcher reputation. A former Yorkshire Academy player, Fletcher junior scooped the Reg Haigh Trophy for the most promising young cricketer of the year (father Stuart won it in 1983). A top opening bowler like his father, in his first full year with

Elland's first team, he scooped 41 wickets at an average of 18.04. His best figures, 5 for 62, came against Clayton West.

Stuart Fletcher is now in charge of a club that is in transition. Without an overseas player, it is down to him to lead the club into a new age with the youngsters.

Slaithwaite's Overseas Professionals
Mark Edmonds

Who were our overseas players, where did they come from, and what have they done since?

Steve Mace. Arriving in 1989 from Australian state side New South Wales, the all-rounder scored over 1,000 runs and took 31 wickets in his first season. *Macey*, as he was affectionately known, stayed for a further four years as the club's overseas professional. The high point was his score of 75 which helped win the 1991 Sykes Cup Final.

Macey was regarded as an honorary *Slawiter*, finishing with a batting average of 42.43. Since returning to *Oz*, Mace has been representing the Charlestown District Cricket Club as Captain.

Drawing by Sue Brant

Pragyan Ojha. The Indian spinner was a *what if* story when he was called up to the Indian Test squad during their tour of England. A tricky left-armer, Ojha then had great success in Zimbabwe and Kenya with the India 'A' side. He was retained in the squad for the visit of the South Africa 'A' team in a series of unofficial Tests and claimed 8 for 97 in the first game.

Even more exciting is playing alongside the world's greatest cricketers for Hyderabad in the Indian Premier League: VVS Laxman, Herschelle Gibbs, Adam Gilchrist, Shahid Afridi, Scott Styris, Andrew Symonds and Chaminda Vaas.

Cameron Cross. Cameron was Slaithwaite's overseas player for 2006. He was the only player to top 1,000 runs for the season, at a superb average of 70.47. He also took 34 wickets.

Cameron has continued his batting form for the Nae Nae Old Boys Cricket Club in the Hazlett Trophy in Wellington, New Zealand.

Top Amateurs

Clive Brook: Mirfield
James Norbury

Clive Brook will be remembered as the Mirfield Captain during the 1963 League and Heavy Woollen Cup *double*, part of the club's golden era between 1958 and 1963, when they lifted the League title four times and the Heavy Woollen Cup twice.

Clive was born in Upper Hopton in 1933 just over the wall from the cricket club and played for the second team in 1946 aged 13. In 1948, he watched Bradman at Headingley score 170 not out on his last tour of the UK.

He played for Mirfield Grammar School between 1946 and 1949 followed by two appearances for Chickenley in the Yorkshire Central League. He had two seasons with Staincliffe, topping the bowling averages with 51 wickets. In 1952 he agreed to join Lascelles Hall and in 1953 switched to Mirfield which had re-formed.

He trained as an engineer and joined the RAF in 1953, working as an air traffic controller at Prestwick Airport. Later, he became a production engineer and eventually changed trades altogether, becoming head of personnel for the same company, Brook Crompton.

In his first Mirfield season, he took six wickets against his former club Chickenley and helped the team to promotion. With Colin Peacock he developed a prolific batting partnership. They became known as the *Mirfield Twins*. Like Clive, Colin Peacock joined the forces, but the partnership re-formed in 1957 and stayed together until the early sixties whilst Mirfield had their purple patch. The dominance ended in 1966 when they were relegated to the second division, though they bounced back the following season.

In 1983, Clive retired after 30 years. His final game was not without incident, however. The scorer dropped his cigarette, igniting a pile of leaves that set the scoring box on fire, "It was at that moment I knew it was time to retire," jokes Clive. In 1987 he made a one-off appearance for the second team because they were short. He took nine wickets in a match-winning performance.

On the committee for much of his playing career, Clive became Vice-Chairman in 1975 and Chairman in 1983, finishing in 1989. In 1995 he was made President of Mirfield Cricket Club, a position he continues in to this day.

Clive remembers his biggest low in 2004 when the club was forced to withdraw from the Bradford League "There was a time when I really thought the club could go under." Thankfully, however, Mirfield was able to sign up to Section 'B' of the Huddersfield League for the following season, immediately gaining promotion to Section 'A'.

Clive looks upon his playing days at Mirfield with great fondness "There is no substitute for walking off that field, realising the entire team have pulled together, and knowing you are all going to have a few drinks afterwards."

Clare Taylor
Peter Redding

Clare Taylor is arguably the most gifted all-round sportswoman that Britain has ever produced, best remembered for her starring role in England's Cricket World Cup triumph in 1993. Two years later, playing football in Sweden, she achieved the unique feat of representing England in World Cups in two different sports.

"I started watching Golcar CC in 1977. John Cooper was the Captain and was my form teacher at Moor End and we thought it would be a laugh to watch him play." Cooper became the first person to recognise her sporting prowess as she warmed up with the team before matches. The following year she agreed to become the scorer for the men's team.

Her first competitive cricket came in 1987 when she played for Wakefield Ladies in the National Premier League. A year later she was wearing the Three Lions: "I was selected to play for Yorkshire in 1987, then at the end of 1988 I was playing in my first World Cup so it was a pretty quick rise up the ranks."

Shortly after her cricket career took off, she moved to play football for Liverpool in the Women's Premier League. She appeared in the Women's FA Cup Final at Wembley in 1995.

Her 26 appearances in Cricket World Cups produced 36 wickets at 13.94 each and an economy rate of 2.1 runs per over. She maintained an economy rate of fewer than 3 over the course of her career "My strength was that I consistently put the ball in the right areas. I always looked to move the ball away from the bat. Sometimes I lacked variation but bowling in the right areas was the key. I wasn't really patient with the bat but I could be with the ball."

After the disappointment of finishing runners-up in her first World Cup, Clare gained her winner's medal in 1993 with 14 wickets, including of 2 for 27 in the Final against New Zealand at Lord's. In 1995 Taylor won a European Championship medal in Dublin, taking 1 for 23 the final against Ireland.

Clare played in three more World Cups (1996, 2000 and 2005). In 2000, with 14 wickets, she was the second most prolific bowler as England reached the Semi-Finals. She made history against Ireland in the 2005 World Cup because, with the wicket of Miriam Grealey, she became the first English woman to take 100 One-Day International wickets. She was the first English woman to play 100 One Day Internationals and is the leading wicket-taker for England. She is third in the overall world list; only Cathryn Fitzpatrick of Australia and Neetu David of India have taken more wickets as of April 2007.

Clare represented England in 16 Test matches, claiming 25 wickets. Her best figures were 4 for 38 against India at Hyderabad in 1995/6. In domestic cricket, she won 11 County Championships in 12 seasons with Yorkshire.

Clare believes that women have become more accepted in the game "When I started, John Cooper and David Thorpe were very support-ive and attitudes towards women playing male sports have improved slightly over the years, but there is still a long way to go as a lot of the national organisations pay lip-service to the women's game rather than really getting behind it. The women's game needs to be successful on the field and have good publicity to keep numbers coming into the game but it is in a fairly healthy state at the moment."

Her services to women's sport were recognised with an MBE in the 2000 Queen's Birthday Honours list "Receiving the MBE from Prince Charles was a very special day. I am a big royalist so I loved all the pageantry and it was great to meet other people who had done amazing things. Being given an MBE was also recognition for women in sport in general."

In October 2006 she became the Women's Cricket Development and Coaching Officer for the Otago State team in New Zealand, ac-cepting a three-year contract, having served as Player/Coach for 2005.

Loyal Copley Duo

Judith Thorpe
Dominic Kureen

Growing up less than five minutes' walk away from Copley with a fa-ther who was addicted to cricket, it was inevitable that Judith Ball, aged 14, began to help her mother with the players' teas. At the same time, brother Ian was beginning his rapid rise through the junior ranks.

During these early years Judith met her future husband, Tom Thorpe, who recalls her passion for the club "The first time that I went for a walk with her she showed me around the ground; it was obvious that it was a fantastic place to play cricket and was close to her heart."

Judith was not content sat at home. She preferred to score, look after the ground and the pavilion, and support. She also possessed a lethal throwing arm "I remember when I used to go down to the ground with Tom and my brother Ian and we'd throw a cricket ball back and forth over the viaduct to each other." That viaduct is a gargantuan structure!

During the 1960s, Judith gave birth to two sons, Andrew and Richard. Despite the responsibility of parenthood, Judith continued to raise funds and help out on match days. Both sons became star players in the Copley side. Richard was one the greatest players ever in the Halifax League, whilst Andrew was a ferocious batsman and a thrilling pace bowler. In 2006, Judith decided to take a breather.

Roy Smith
Dominic Kureen

As you walk through Copley's pavilion your eye will be drawn to a silver plaque with a picture of Roy and his wife, Barbara. It lists his club achievements, concluding "In Halifax he was known as *Mr Cricket*; in Yorkshire he was known as *Mr Halifax*. There can be no better accolade."

Roy was a member of Copley from 1927 to his death in 1997. A top quality wicketkeeper and aggressive opening batsman, he won the Copley fielding prize no less than ten times (a club record) and the batting prize on seven occasions.

He was a committee member from 1929, Chairman from 1955 to 1965 and Club President between 1965 and 1997. He was Copley's league representative from 1936 to 1953, President of the Halifax League between 1971 and 1988 and a White Rose committee member. He was also responsible for establishing the successful Halifax Junior League.

He was an inspiration, as Tom Thorpe recalls "Roy was an aggressive batsman and an aggressive captain. One of my outstanding memories of him on the cricket field was that he was one of the first players who I saw hit a century for Copley. I was a teenager, opening the batting with him and I got a duck. A hundred was quite a feat back then on poorly cared-for pitches of inconsistent bounce and long grass."

Current first-team star Tim Rushton also benefited from Roy's presence "He was a great character both on and off the pitch and Copley through and through. He did a lot for Copley, the Halifax League and local cricket in general."

(Copley was formed in 1880 and play in the Halifax League)

Last Man Out
Lee Hughes (Ms)

Crossing the cool of the green village grass
Evokes memories so special, too fragile to last
The worn and torn pitch from the matches we played
Reminders of victories on hot summer days

Pictures of practising in a soldier's regime
Aspiring for victory in the war at the seam
Walking away I'm pulled back once more
But the season is over it's time to retire

The hour to surrender now autumn moves on
All battles are through, the last game is won
But my heart and my soul are already at home
As I stand on this pitch in my *whites* all alone

Long Serving Clubmen

Harry Andrew: Northowram Hedge Top
Jon O'Shea

Harry Andrew's long career began as a medium-pace bowler with Bradshaw's U18s. He took 7 for 2 runs against Halifax YMCA, and 9 for 16 versus Ovenden.

He left in 1959, aged 30, to live in Bradford and joined Hedge Top. He made his first 50 for Bradshaw at the ground and considered it a "fine batting wicket."

The side had been struggling in the second division of the Halifax League and funds were dangerously low. Fortunately, the arrival of players such as Harry and the late left-arm quick Alan Kellett, provided a sharp uplift in fortunes. The club bought the Hedge Top Lane premises, which they had previously leased from the Coley Trust, for the then considerable sum of £600.

Harry captained the fast-improving First XI to second division glory in 1962. In 1965 they reached the Final of the Halifax Parish Cup. Harry was part of the eleven which overcame favourites Triangle thanks to Kellett's resourceful bowling and skipper Alan Butterworth's unbeaten 31. They were Halifax League Division One champions the following year, unbeaten throughout the season.

Harry was appointed Club Secretary under the tutelage of de facto Club President Walter Howden, but quickly progressed to Treasurer, a post he held for 30 years. In 1998, Harry became Club President. He oversaw the construction of a brick pavilion, later extended to include showering, toilet and finally, bar facilities. In the early 1990s, as head groundsman, he helped relay five playing wickets and add five new practice strips. He has since introduced a purpose-built scoring unit and sliding sightscreens.

(Northowram Hedge Top was formed in 1919 as Northowram Wesleyans)

Keith Hudson: Bridgeholme

Brian Heywood

Keith was just 21 when he and Peter Brennand took over as grounds-men in 1985. The club was at a low ebb. All clubs suffer from internal politics and occasionally major rifts. At the end of 1984 Bridgeholme lost several key players. After two decades of steady progress, both team and ground were in decline and the club was compelled to resign from the Halifax League. They returned to the Halifax Association's third division, back where they were in 1964. The club re-built and went back to the Halifax League in 2001.

On Sunday Keith sweeps the used wicket from Saturday and repairs it by re-seeding the ends and levelling them off. He then begins work on the pitch for the following week, brushing up the grass, cutting and rolling it for half an hour. The rolling is repeated every evening and the pitch receives two further cuts, one midweek and one on Friday, when it is also marked out. Saturday morning is kept in reserve in case of bad weather, but the pitch always receives a final roll and the square is trimmed, the stripes enhancing the ground's aesthetic appeal.

Keith is often working on the ground whilst his team mates are knock-ing up and he sometimes opens the batting on a pitch he was rolling only ten minutes earlier. Occasionally this lack of mental and physical preparation contributes to an early dismissal, but it can't happen too often as he has accumulated around 500 runs per season on a pretty regular basis since the early 1990s.

In September Keith scarifies and re-seeds. The scarifying machine is usually hired, although Walsden Cricket Club have kindly lent their ma-chine recently. He applies a top-dressing of fifty 25 kg bags of Mendip Loam, eight each to the five pitches on the square and eight to the U18s track. It's back-breaking work and takes a full weekend to complete. After that, seeds are scattered liberally.

During the winter the outfield is cut roughly once a month. At week-ends Keith and co-groundsman Peter Brennand usually work on their latest project, which could be anything from repairing a sightscreen to cleaning out the guttering.

The arrival of Spring and attention returns to the playing area. The outfield is cut twice weekly in the run-up to the season and the square receives much brushing, cutting and rolling.

As Bridgeholme's Chairman and league representative, Keith has many administrative duties. It concerns Keith that the club is run by just a handful of loyal members and confesses it would be healthier to have the load spread more widely. They are unimpeded by bureaucracy, however, and make and implement decisions quickly and efficiently.

Keith's ability to make sound, fair judgements was recognised in 2002 when he was asked to join the executive of the Halifax League.

Dave Evans: Bradshaw
Zak Data

Dave Evans is the groundsman at Bradshaw Cricket Club. Now in his mid 70s, Dave has been voluntarily helping out at Bradshaw for over 50 years.

Dave started playing cricket at school. A budding all-rounder, Dave settled as bowler. He proudly says he ran out of space on his mantel-piece for all his awards and trophies! His favourite trophy is the league bowling prize.

Nowadays, groundsmen can take ECB and Institute of Groundsmen day courses. Dave has attended some. "These courses are very well put together for people like myself and up and coming groundsmen. There is always something new you can learn and if you are willing to learn you will definitely develop as a groundsman. Plus I have had the opportunity to tour Headingley Cricket Ground which was a dream come true."

In conjunction with his role as groundsman, Dave is also the club's Treasurer. He has sole responsibility for keeping the club's finances in order and for stocking up on beer and wine.

Dave doesn't have many hobbies outside helping Bradshaw Cricket Club. He has a fondness for travel and is a strong family man, spending most of his free time with his children and grandchildren.

Dave explains how it is very important to remain enthusiastic if you want to have longevity as a groundsman. "My advice to future grounds-men is that you should try enrolling on a groundsmanship course. It teaches you the basics of being a groundsman."

Dave would like nothing more than to take on a young apprentice. He confesses, "I have a young lad I am training at the moment. It is really rewarding passing on my knowledge and expertise."

The Heights of Bradshaw
Mark Whitcombe

I sighed in relief as I saw the old parish church. We were on Bradshaw Lane. It was only a matter of moments later when we saw Bradshaw cricket ground. High up, it is home to a wonderful view. Hills gently rear up in the distance, creating the backdrop for fields showing the hard labour of farmers.

We are high. Higher than most grounds around our little cricketing area. If you look over the scorebox you see the hill edge, slanting like a great cliff. It is a silhouette against the sky.

Standing and staring, breathing in the air and taking in the view and the sun beating down hard. Come winter the clouds will gather and the club will quiver under the snow. In autumn there will be colours of gold and brown, the trees will shake their leaves and the sky will fall down in crashing storms. Spring will bring change and new life, a colour to the trees, a vibrancy to the air.

(Bradshaw began in 1923 and play in the Halifax League)

Barry Tennyson: Barkisland
Mark Edmonds

Originally from neighbouring village Crumlin, Barry joined Barkisland in 1949 as a ten-year old junior, following in the footsteps of both his older brother Terry who was primarily a batsman, and his father who was the club's scorer.

He left aged 18, unable to gain a place in the First XI. Two years later he returned and was immediately made captain. Things went well until a loss against rivals Greetland. "Harry Schofield blamed my captaincy for the defeat," says Barry, with a wry smile on his face. "At that point, I didn't think I had to put up with criticism like that, so I left at the end of that season to go to Sowerby."

After a two-year sabbatical, he spent the rest of his playing career at the club. Again as Captain, Barry led Barkisland to Parish Cup victories in 1977, 1978, 1979 and 1984. He was also part of the sides that won the Parish Cup in both 1981 and 1987 as well as a member of the Crossley Shield-winning team of 1957 with his brother Terry.

In 1987, he took a place on the committee. "I'm still very involved with the game, and especially with Barkisland. Every weekend of the season I'm umpiring a game in the league as the club's representative. I didn't realise just how difficult the job was before I started though!" He is also club trustee and represents them at Sunday Section meetings. In 1992 he was made Chairman of the Halifax Cricket League, a position he is very proud to hold.

George Bottomley: Lightcliffe
Zak Data

George Bottomley died recently, aged 92. He gave outstanding service to Lightcliffe during a 75 year association with the club.

He was a star all-rounder who featured in the Priestley Cup victories of 1937 and 1950. He had short spells playing professional cricket, especially with Pudsey St Lawrence in 1955. In that season Lightcliffe defeated the Saints by four wickets in the Priestley Cup Final.

In 1963 he joined the club's committee. He was Chairman from the early 1980s until 1998. His outstanding contribution was acknowledged in 1995 when he received the Bradford League's coveted award, the Sir Leonard Hutton Trophy.

George was also a fine footballer. This caught the attention of Arsenal who offered the chance to play for them under their legendary manager Herbert Chapman. Close family members persuaded him to follow a career with a local carpet manufacturer instead. He also played golf at Cleckheaton Golf Club and was a member of the Old Brodleians Rugby Union Club.

Lightcliffe Chairman Bruce Lunn said, "If you had the luxury of meeting George, you would automatically realise what an astonishing man he was. He had a larger than life personality, which rubbed off on everyone he met. He gave so much to the club as a player and as a supporter."

(Lightcliffe were formed in 1875 and play in the Bradford League)

Tranquillity at Lightcliffe
Mark Whitcombe

I like the scene before me. It is red. In the middle of green. The fields are lush and full of vibrant life. The wind rushes through them, rippling towards the tranquillity at Lightcliffe Cricket Club. Like so many of these rich relics bathed in serenity, the ground is hidden away, enclosed by the country air. I find myself immersed in a daydream. I want to stay here. I want to play here. The setting is so perfect. Everything is so clean. So together. So right.

Lightcliffe is set in another world, up a lane enclosed between two fields. You cannot ignore the trees that cluster around, green and high, shaking in the wind, radiant in the sun. Nor can you ignore the great church close by, foundations old and flag flying high. And then of course there is that tower. That structure standing high as you enter the ground. I marvel at its existence. That red pavilion where a clock is placed, recording time. The scorer's box standing alone, watching patiently. The presence of huts storing the tools for the groundsman. Then there is that little shed next to the old pavilion. On it there is sign saying umpires. It seems that nobody is forgotten.

Timeless

Mick Baldwin: Gomersal
Zak Data

Mick Baldwin has been Chairman of Gomersal since 2005. Before that he was at Hartshead Moor where his father is the groundsman and his brother is Chairman.

Mick started playing cricket at the age of 8. 38 years later he looks back on his successful career: "I thought I was a terrific player. But some of my colleges would beg to differ," he laughs. "Unfortunately I haven't won any team trophies, but I have won a few fielding trophies."

The club has 500 members. The clubhouse is located in the middle of the village and Mick boasts that the bar is by far the best in the village, regularly holding weddings, birthdays, fun days and discos.

Mick is proud that cricket is played daily on the Gomersal ground. In addition to the two senior teams, the club have U9, U11, U12, U13, two U15 and U17 teams. He believes the club can maintain their dominance in future "If the first team stay in the first league it is an incentive for the younger stars of tomorrow. Good coaching and nurturing them in the correct manner is vital."

(Gomersal is a Bradford League club, beginning as Gomersal St Mary's in 1881)

Nortonthorpe Collection

A Lifetime at Nortonthorpe: Norman Mosley
Matt Ottey

At the age of 15 Norman started playing cricket, taking a fancy to batting. Kenneth Armitage, opened with Norman throughout Nortonthorpe's *Golden Years*. "We were together while we were playing as kids, then we moved into the seconds before both making our way into the firsts. There was an understanding, we didn't get a lot of run out's!" They helped clinch 5 league titles and 3 Allsop Cup Final victories.

Still, as Norman prepared to hang up his pads, he was unexpectedly being sized up for an umpiring role by fellow player Rowland Hardy. In a cunning plan involving constant ear-bashing and copious amounts of alcohol, Hardy set his plans in motion, as Norman explains "Me and a few of the other players were in the pub one night. We hadn't been in there for very long when Rowland came over and asked me to umpire a game for him the next day. I told him in not so many words to bugger off, but throughout the night he kept asking me to do it, buying me drinks and the like. So eventually, when I'd had enough to drink, I gave in and told him I'd do it, apparently."

And so with one drink too many started a lengthy umpiring career. Recalling his early days "For the first season or so I was a bit shaky, worrying about decisions, about keeping discipline and missing things, but eventually you learn to just call what you see. I remember one match during my first season when the players were appealing for everything. I was umpiring with a fella who had been about a bit, so the next time they appealed he called me over, offered me a mint and said 'Don't turn around, they'll think we're talking about 'em, scare 'em to death'. And it worked!"

Norman is still umpiring with Nortonthorpe and during the cricket season regularly tours the country watching his favourite sport. "I go as far north as Chester-le-Street (Durham) and as far south as Grace Road (Leicestershire)."

Springfield Avenue
Daniel Stewart

The size of Nortonthorpe's cricket ground is impressive. The pavilion looks small in comparison, swamped by the sea of green beyond it. Around the manicured pitch is a curtain of soft trees. The views are phenomenal. The focal point is the Emley Moor mast. The panorama of the valley and hills beyond make the pitch seem more like a vantage point from which you can watch the world go by.

A Good Friendly Atmosphere
Matt Hayes, Nortonthorpe
Matt Ottey

When did your club website go online?

Some time around July 2006.

How many people help with the website apart from you?

I do all the updating. However, Helen Sansom has provided many photos and Pete Spark writes most of our match reports.

What are your main day-to-day tasks as webmaster?

Updating the averages and results. Currently trying to get old score-cards on there.

Which features of the site are most popular?

Match reports and averages mainly.

How might your website develop in the future?

I would like to get a players section on there with profiles.

In your opinion, what is special and unique about your club?

Just a good friendly atmosphere and people who don't take cricket too seriously.

Favourite away ground you like visiting?

Cawthorne, my old team.

What has changed most about local cricket during your lifetime?

Not been playing for too long yet but it's good to see more young-sters getting a game on a Saturday.

Meet Adrian Whittaker
Servant of Club and League
Matt Ottey

Adrian Whittaker was born and raised in Clayton West, next door to Scissett, and like most young cricket enthusiasts obtained his first posi-tion in the game as a scorer at 10 years of age for Clayton West.

His rise from scorer to player was rapid and exciting, getting himself into the Second XI at the age of just 14. The promotion from second to

first team was even quicker, playing his first match at 16. He went on to win 13 league championships between 1967 and 1996, six under his captaincy.

He also appeared in six Allsop Cup Finals, winning only the once.

In the late 1980s he joined the league management board, and became Vice President in the early 1990s. He took over as President of the Huddersfield Central league 14 years ago, standing down at November's AGM in 2007 because Clayton West decided to move into the Huddersfield Drakes League.

"Having played at Nortonthorpe on a number of occasions, I knew they were struggling both on and off the field. They had very little funds and only one team." Clearly Adrian thought he could help.

"I approached Roy England, Roger and Brian and said I would come on board to start a Second XI, write to businesses for ball sponsorship, sponsor the fixture card and be the groundsman." Roy England puts it "Since he's come in to help us out he's done a fantastic job with the ground."

In 2002 he started an U13s 8-a-side junior team which ran for 3 years before having to disband. "Unfortunately once the players moved up to U15s we needed 11 players, and due to the size of the village, school trips and the kids' holidays, it meant we were always missing 3 or 4."

In 2007 he was made a life member of the League, and at the Annual Dinner in March the following year was deservedly awarded the League's Stallard Trophy for his services to cricket.

(Formed in 1877, Nortonthorpe play in the Huddersfield Central League)

Timeless

Shepley Partnership

Geoff Gill
Dave Wooding

A man who was at the heart of the Shepley team for many years, former club Captain Geoff Gill commanded immense respect from all those around him, during a playing career that spanned over 25 years, most of which were spent at Shepley,

Starting his cricketing life as a bowler, Geoff made his senior bow at 15, for Lascelles Hall, where he proudly recalls, "I managed to take a wicket with my first ever ball." Despite opening the bowling once for the Yorkshire's U18s, injuries eventually forced him to concentrate on batting.

Geoff joined Shepley for the 1977 season. Apart from two years at Batley in 1980 and 1981, Shepley was Geoff's home club until 2003. During his first Batley season he was awarded the batting trophy for the Central Yorkshire League.

Perhaps the biggest hitter in Shepley history, Geoff admits "I never really did a lot of running between the wickets. I preferred hitting sixes!" His highest score was 208 against local rivals Shelley, and he recalls "I hit 16 sixes and 14 fours in that knock."

Despite obvious individual ability, Geoff enjoyed playing for the team. He says, "If I get runs it's nice, but if we win and I get nothing I'm still happy." With this attitude, coupled with a natural cricketing brain, it was perhaps little surprise when Geoff took over as Captain during 1984.

Geoff describes himself as "a very focused captain" who was not afraid to make controversial and difficult decisions to help lead his team to victory. He would make his decisions and then expect his players to either "like it or lump it, regardless of who they were." Indeed, during his time in charge he was known to replace bowlers after just one over if they failed to live up to expectations.

The 1984 team was tipped for relegation in the *Examiner's* season preview, yet they took the title. With by no means the most talented team of cricketers at his disposal, Geoff and his side defied the odds, something he puts down to the closeness and the attitude of the team. They won several matches that could have gone either way. Indeed, with no batsman averaging over 30, it took a great team effort and Geoff's captaincy played its part. He says, "It will probably never be done again with a team like ours was that year."

Those around the club will remember the infamous incident involving Derek Randall, the former England international, who felt the full brunt of Geoff's professionalism in a Sykes Cup match between Shepley and Randall's Thongsbridge. While it may seem to have been a controversial decision to inform Randall that he was not allowed to bat because he had missed the previous day's action, Geoff, ever the team player, was quick to consult his colleagues before being placed in the unenviable position of making the tough, but ultimately correct, decision.

Geoff singles out leading the Huddersfield League U22s to victory in the prestigious White Rose competition as one of his greatest moments. It was Shepley who probably gave Geoff his lowest moment in cricket, as he was part of the team that suffered relegation in 1997, as well as being a losing finalist in the 1990 Heavy Woollen Cup.

Ray Horrocks
Dave Wooding

"The biggest mistake most people make is thinking that groundsmen have the winter off!" states Ray Horrocks, Shepley's long standing groundsman. "What you put into the pitch in terms of effort and work in the winter, you will get out in the summer."

Reseeding all the footmarks left by the bowlers is just one of the tasks

Timeless

when the season ends. It cannot be done during the summer, as there is no time for grass to grow. The grass on the square must be trimmed, "If you don't keep the grass at a certain length, it can easily become diseased." Aerating the grass with either his spiking or slitting machine is another integral part of his winter programme. Ray explains that the process will improve the roots, and help them get access to the water that allows them to grow healthily.

With the season around six weeks away, using systematic worm casts, he is able to force the local worms to burrow deeper into the ground, as opposed to leaving wormholes on his square. This is followed a week or so later by treating the grass on the square with lawn sand to prevent moss emerging during the season.

Ray then brings the roller out of its winter retirement. One of the little known tricks of the trade that Ray employs at this stage is to first roll across the wicket instead of up and down it. The aim here is to ensure the surface remains even. Following this first roll, Ray estimates that the square at Shepley, "probably gets around 15 hours of rolling time before the season starts."

Surely then, it must be heartbreaking as the players take to the field with cricket spikes damaging all that he has worked hard to create? Well, as Ray puts it "My satisfaction comes from seeing a good game of cricket on a nice white wicket. It can be a bugger when it goes wrong and we lose, because a lot of people want to point the finger at the wicket."

(Shepley began in 1871 and play in the Huddersfield League)

Skelmanthorpe Collection

Committed to the Cause: Trevor Heeley
Matt Elston

Awarded the prestigious Fred Stallard Trophy for services to local cricket, Trevor Heeley is one of the most committed individuals in the game. Former RAF man Trevor, a reluctant flyer who served on the ground, occasionally dabbled in table tennis but later became more than fully involved with cricket.

He spent the 1950s and 1960s keeping Skelmanthorpe alive. He's been a player, league representative for an incredible 50 years, Secretary for 37 years and the club's youngest ever Chairman. He turned his hand to umpiring and is still campaigning to get young umpires into the local leagues. He organises league and cup fixtures, winter nets, general meetings and training, spending his entire life working with and for Skelmanthorpe, as dedicated now as he was at the club AGM 55 years ago.

Trevor's campaigns against rate relief for amateur clubs are well known. He continually strives to get the best for the club and local community. Trevor is also a regular member of his church and plays the piano accordion.

He considers himself to have been "privileged and honoured" to contribute so much to Huddersfield cricket.

Margaret Dollive
Matt Elston

In 1998 Margaret Dollive and Beverley Crossland became Skelmanthorpe's Chair and Vice-Chair respectively.

Margaret's involvement began as a junior league scorer, watching her sons Adam and James play three times a week. Eighteen years on, she has been active in the Ladies Committee, fund raising for the team, decorating the clubhouse and ultimately sitting as Chair on the Committee.

The club stresses the importance of local young talent like Max Joice, Kristian Whittaker and James Crossland "We have good enough players who could play anywhere in the Huddersfield League and earn good money, but the local lads are really loyal and have stuck with us."

Local support is important without which the club would surely perish. 'It's a compliment to the cricket club that so many people support us,' she says.

Phil Redgwick: Shat's Own *Ground Force*
Matthew Elston

Wind, rain, sleet, snow and the occasional day of sunlight, nothing keeps this weathered campaigner from his square. Whether he's tending to the wicket or taking care of the opposition's opening bowlers, *Redgy* never lacks commitment. A gruff-accented opening batsman, raised on nearby Lidget Lane, he is as Skelmanthorpe, or *Shat*, as they come.

Redgy's rough features are unmistakeable; a face worn by the wind and slightly tinted by the sun and characteristic of a local cricket groundsman. Phil has been with Skelmanthorpe since 1980, tending to the field since 1988 and groundsman at the Galpharm Stadium for four years.

Allegedly an opening bat, Redgwick looks back on a fantastic career at Skelmanthorpe. One of his finest memories was the 1990 League and Sykes Cup double; their first-ever Sykes Cup success after being only a whisker away on three previous occasions. He recalls celebrations so memorable they left him "crawling out of the clubhouse on my hands and knees."

Redgwick is clearly a big favourite in the village and has enjoyed more than his fair share of successes, little wonder with players like Mahboob, Irani, Hurlbatt and Higgins for company.

Despite time not being on his side, and "not being as quick as I used to be," he wants to be with the Lidget Lane club long into his twilight years.

(Skelmanthorpe was formed in 1871 and play in the Huddersfield League)

Meltham Partnership

One Swallow Makes a Summer:
16 Years at Meltham
Rob Hardie

Since making his debut for Meltham against Holmfirth on the 25 April 1992 Ian Swallow has given 16 years of dedicated service.

Before then, Ian played 88 first-class matches in eight years with Yorkshire and Somerset. He hit 1,550 runs at an average of 20.39, including two half-centuries and a highest score of 114. His right arm off-breaks took 106 wickets with an economy rate of 3.10.

During his time at Meltham (ten years as Captain) the club won over ten titles. Ian captured four personal awards including the Clifford Sykes Cup for most league catches in 1996, the Jack Gledhill Memorial Trophy for the best all-rounder of 2000, and Man of the Match (1994, 1997) in two of four Sykes Cup Finals.

Between 1992 and 2001, Ian skippered Meltham to the Byrom Shield and the Sykes Cup four times apiece, the Yorkshire Championship twice and the Huddersfield League Conference Championship.

2000 was a marvellous season. He averaged 46.58 with the bat from 23 innings including 4 not outs and a top score of 101 not out. He bowled 260 overs, 53 maidens, 49 wickets, an economy rate of 2.75 and took 14 catches.

In 2005, Ian hit over 1,000 runs from 24 innings, finishing with his best ever seasonal average of 50.25, including a career highest of 122 not out.

Ian Swallow played his final game for Meltham away to Honley on 15 September 2007. His club totals were 13,706 runs at an average of 38.50 and 482 wickets with an economy rate of 3.28.

Charles Edwin Robson: "I try to get as many people involved with the club"
Rob Hardie

The current President of Meltham Cricket Club is Charles Edwin Robson, a plumber and gas fitter from Holmfirth who has been involved with the club for over 30 years.

What are your primary roles?

I try to get as many people involved in the club and attend as many functions as I can. I listen to what people have to say and keep the club running smoothly by sorting out any problems that arise.

What were your thoughts on the club's performance last season?

Frustrating. The weather didn't help. Although well done to the stiffs for winning the Paddock Shield!

What sort of players do the club need to look to bring in?

We're short of a good bowler, but everybody is. We need some batters who are prepared to work hard and forge out an innings and not just thrash out. Hopefully, some of our younger players will knuckle down and show us that they can do it.

How important is the Second XI to the club?

The Second XI gives our better youngsters a chance to play at a higher level. It keeps the older players from under their wives' feet! The Second XI is a hard team to handle, matching old and young together, winning matches and also losing players to the first team.

How important are the youth teams to the club?

They are important as they bring in youngsters and get them involved in a team sport, gaining experience through working together.

Favourite cricketer?

The one and only Ian Swallow. What he's done for this club is well documented and he will be a hard cricketer to replace both on and off the field.

Favourite sports outside cricket?

I'm a season ticket-holder at Huddersfield Town.

(Meltham was established in 1867 and plays in the Huddersfield League)

Miscellany

Caught between the stumps and the goalposts
Ian Hirst

Sportsmen are always put in tricky positions. There are club versus country rows and whether or not to play despite carrying an injury. What happens if they cross into two different sports?

Sean Mee, a cricket player for Broad Oak and a football player for Linthwaite:

> The season overlaps two weeks around May. It means some teams suffer from players like me who have to play one or the other and are vital pieces in both sides. Really, it should be changed. I don't know what could be done. Possibly playing more Sunday games in cricket and mid week games in football.

Frank Beaumont, President of the Huddersfield and District Association Football League, who has been involved with the League for over 40 years, explained the current rule:

> If both teams agree to switch their match to a mid week game and before the match was scheduled for, then there is no problem with that. There were discussions in the 1970s about having the mid-week games at the start of the season but there were still problems and difficulties.

Roger France, the chairman of the Drakes Huddersfield Cricket League:

> When I played football it was nowhere as serious as it is now. Some coaches think they are managing Man United. They organise friendly matches on Saturdays, still knowing that many players will be playing cricket. Truthfully there is not a lot we can do. There is pressure on me to make the season longer but

that would just cause more problems. We can't expand the season and we can't reduce the season either, as there is just not enough dates. There are already enough Saturday and Sunday matches, and teams, especially the second string, struggle to pull a side together. In an ideal world players would honour their commitments with the clubs they are playing for. It is down to them at the end of the day.

There seems to be no solution, so sportsmen will just have to choose.

Gower, Wasim and Moonraking:
11 Things You Might Not Have Known About Slaithwaite CC
Mark Edmonds

Edwin St. Hill was the first black cricketer to represent any side in the Huddersfield League. He made his debut for Slaithwaite in 1934 after being introduced to the club by the legendary Learie Constantine.

Why is the club badge so? Mythology has it that local smugglers tried to explain their nocturnal activities as "raking the moon from the canal." As a result *Moonraker* is now the official nickname for a native of the village.

Tom Simpson took two hat-tricks in the same season for Slaithwaite's second string in 2006. Bowling medium-paced in-swingers, Simpson took all his wickets either by lbw, caught by the wicketkeeper or caught and bowled.

England star Ryan Sidebottom pitted his wits as a teenager against current *Slawit* player John Hey in two different matches. Once when Hey was at Holmfirth as they played Meltham, and the other when Sidebottom represented Kirkburton against Linthwaite.

Hey also had the privilege of taking on Ryan Sidebottom's father Arnie, himself an England Test cricketer, when Primrose Hill played Slaithwaite.

Current first-teamer Dave Berry managed to send current India opening batsman Wasim Jaffer into a spin while the international was at

Scholes. Not only did Berry take Jaffer's wicket caught and bowled, he also had two extremely good shouts for gloved behind and an lbw turned down. To this day, Berry maintains he got him out three times!

Sun, of all things, rather than 'rain, stopped play' has been known to occur on occasions due to the sun setting down by the scoreboard, blinding both players and umpires.

As a teenager, England legend David Gower was turned down by Slaithwaite! Leicestershire sent three players up for experience but SCC only needed two. As a result, Dave Munden, who is now a professional sports photographer, and Tim Smith, who went on to play for various minor counties, were chosen at Gower's expense.

In 1987, the club entered, and then went on to win, the Heavy Woollen Cup at the very first time of asking, defeating Chickenley by 41 runs. SCC also reached the final in 1991 and 1993.

Yorkshire all-rounder Craig White was part of the Honley side that played Slaithwaite in 1991. The ex-England player starred as the two teams clashed in the Sykes Cup Final held at Slaithwaite. Slaithwaite won the trophy that year.

Bank Holiday weekend in May 2005 saw not one but two centuries from Chris Payne, both against Meltham, one at home and one away, with scores of 169 on the Saturday and 121 on the Sunday!

A Golcar *All-Star XI:*
Thorpey celebrates 30 years at the Lilies
Peter Redding

2007 marks the 125th anniversary of the year that St. John's Golcar became Golcar Cricket Club. It has become a popular trend to pick all-time elevens. They provoke great debate because it is hard to compare players from different eras. David Thorpe's association with *The Lilies* dates back to 1977 as a young batsmen making his way in the Second XI. *Thorpey* spent a decade in the first team up until his retirement in the late 1980s since when he has been a regular viewer at Swallow Lane, helping coach the younger age groups. He told me the criteria that he had used to pick his *Dream Team*, "The first thing to stress is that I have picked the best team and not the best 11 cricketers … I have tried to pick a balanced team of overseas players and local lads."

So here is David Thorpe's All Star Golcar XI:

John Cooper (1968-2004). Opening batsmen who played the anchorman role. He became the leading run scorer in the history of the Huddersfield League. "He was a steady accumulator of runs and he had a good temperament. He gives the team the right balance because you need batsmen that are prepared to bat for a long time as well as players that attack."

Prakash Karkera (1989-1990). Indian first-class cricketer in the late 1980s. "Had more shots than John Cooper but you would expect that seeing as he was a first-class cricketer; he was capable of making big hundreds." Scored eight centuries during his two seasons.

Steve Whitwam (1995-2000, 2005-present). Scored his maiden century at the age of 16. "Steve has more shots than most of the batsmen and he is also a handy off-spin bowler." Best all-rounder title in the Huddersfield League for the past two seasons.

Shane Deitz (1995). "Shane only played for Golcar for one season when he wasn't training with South Australia; he didn't actually keep wicket at the club because he wanted to bowl." Hit four centuries. Aggressive left-handed batsman, still plying his trade with South Australia.

Atul Bedade (1999-2004). "Atul would be picked for his entertainment value alone; he was known in India for his ability to hit sixes and he didn't treat bowlers with much respect. His weakness was probably that he often got bored particularly against lesser sides; he was more motivated by the bigger occasions." Best remembered for his mammoth innings of 234 not out against Hall Bower in the Sykes Cup. Scored over 3,000 first class runs for Baroda in India.

Sanjeev Sharma (1987-1988). "Sanjeev was predominantly a bowler, he perhaps didn't put himself forward enough. I remember a game when he was reluctant to bat but he went in early and he was by far our best batsman." Best remembered for taking two nine-wicket hauls against Bradley Mills and Lockwood. Also famous for being the bowler who had Graham Gooch dropped early at Lords in 1990; Gooch went on to make 333.

Kevin Plant (early 1980s). "Kevin was an excellent cover-point fielder; he would save about 20 runs in some games and he was an excellent athlete because he played at stand-off for the Yorkshire county rugby team. He was also a PE teacher. He once got injured playing in a rugby final and it kept him out of some of the cricket that season, I don't think some people were happy about that! He was a fielder who the opposition were always wary of and they were frightened to run when the ball went anywhere near him."

Phil Eastwood (early 1990s). "Phil came through the junior team, he's a local lad. He was an all-rounder who bowled right-arm medium pace. He went on to captain Slaithwaite."

Bruce Jakeman (late 1980s). "Bruce started off at Holmbridge at a very young age; he was something of a young prodigy. He came over to Golcar towards the end of his career and he was very enthusiastic."

Brian Turner (1968-1982). "Brian took well over 1,000 wickets in the Huddersfield League. He came to Golcar from Sheffield United. He was a bowler who attacked no matter what the situation was. I remember a match against Lascelles Hall where they needed six to win off the last ball. In that situation most bowlers would try and bowl it as wide as possible or at leg stump but Brian tried to take a wicket and that was his attitude, he wanted to take a wicket off every ball; in the end the lad hit a six and we lost that game." Well known for his skilled use of the slope at Swallow Lane, like Glenn McGrath at Lord's. Also played two matches for Yorkshire and with combined figures of 4 for 47 he was unlucky not to play more.

Jasbir Singh (mid 1980s). "Jasbir was an old fashioned slow left-arm bowler with a classical action. He was very reminiscent of Monty Panesar both in his action and his appearance because he was a Sikh and he always wore a turban. He has since gone on to become an umpire and he has officiated in six One Day Internationals." Took 96 first-class wickets during his career at an impressive 24.50 apiece.

Shepley's Best-Ever XI?
Dave Wooding

Geoff Gill. Surely the most fitting candidate for the role of captain. Geoff spent in excess of 20 years at Marsh Lane, and was skipper for several, leading the team to the Byrom Shield title in 1984. Geoff had a fine cricketing brain and is one of the most respected captains in Shepley history. With a big-hitting batting style, Geoff has hit more sixes than anyone else ever to play at Shepley.

Paul Dyson. In the early 1990s, Australian right-handed batsman, Paul Dyson, passed the 1,000 run mark on two occasions in his three seasons. Dale Skelly recalls the memorable knock against Skelmanthorpe when Dyson scored 150, and "we still managed to lose somehow!" Paul was one of the few overseas players to settle off the field as well as on it.

Dale Skelly. Former captain Brian Kettlewell describes Dale as "probably the best keeper we've had at Shepley." He spent more than ten seasons behind the stumps and once faced competition from the son of a rich investor looking to pump money into the club. Dale was too good to drop and the investor pulled out. An integral part of Geoff Gill's Byrom Shield-winning side in 1984, Dale was also a useful opening batsman.

Neil Jurgenson. Of the many good Shepley overseas players perhaps *Jurgy* was the most talented. He joined in 1981, scoring a quick century on debut. A series of further big scores and *Jurgy* became the first player in seven years to pass the 1,000 run mark in the Drakes Huddersfield League. The South African top-order batsman was part of the side that won the Byrom Shield in 1982. Former teammate Brian Kettlewell described him "as good a batter as I've seen in a long time."

Ian Glover. Shepley's master swing bowler and stunning catcher was part of Geoff Gill's title-winning team in 1984. Included in the Huddersfield Cricket League representative team on several occasions in the early 1980s, alongside Neil Jurgenson.

Phil Heaton. Current club captain with great commitment, commuting from Bury to Shepley for the last 14 seasons. A left-handed all-rounder. Phil headed the bowling averages last season with 40 victims.

Colin Shaw. Colin was a feared opening bowler and a lower-middle order batsman who could bat from time to time. Originally from Meltham, he is another strong candidate for best captain, as Trevor Curtis recalls, "a very respected captain at Marsh Lane."

David Cocking. David began at Shepley in the 1970s, joining from Denby Dale in the Central League. Trevor Curtis says, "He was the sort of bowler who could hold up an end, bowling 20 or so overs and concede only about 30 runs." Cocking's tall stature lead to an unorthodox batting style, often fooling bowlers into thinking they had an easy victim.

Steve Carter. Another import from the Huddersfield Central League. A steady bowler (often used as first change) and a calculating batsman. He always knew exactly how many runs were required and once walked off having won a match and the umpires had to be told that Shepley had actually reached their target!

David *Corky* Beaumont. Left-arm spin bowler, Beaumont has won many games for Shepley with his flight. Another good tactician; a former captain of the Huddersfield League representative team in the 1980s.

Brian Kettlewell. Highly assured player, reliable top-order batsman, now a league umpire, and another of Shepley's former captains. Started as a *pro* at Kirkburton, before moving to Thurstonland. Picked for the league representative side whilst at Shepley.

Darren Gough. Arguably the most talented cricketer ever to play for Shepley, Gough established himself in the England Test side between the mid 1990s and 2003, continuing then in One Day Internationals.

Adrian Guy. Another player from Meltham. Adrian put the ball in the right spot and frustrated batsmen. He scored the winning runs in one of Shepley's most memorable victories against rivals Skelmanthorpe, hitting a six off the last ball.

Howard Palmer. A talented all-rounder, Howard used to open in the 1970s, and still plays for the Second XI at Meltham. As a youth, Howard made a few appearances for the Yorkshire Colts Second XI.

Raju Kulkane. Talented Indian all-rounder who spent a season at Shepley. Captained his home-town side of Bombay and played three Test matches in 1986 and 1987. Despite perhaps not integrating as well as other overseas players have, he was certainly a valuable asset to the club when he was on top of his game.

Interlude - IV
The Final that Took Weeks and Weekes Victory
Allan Stuttard

On August 30 Walsden suspended at 150 for 6. Middleton went in again and, on August 31, were finally all out for 220. Walsden pushed on and were 194 when Jim was out, caught at silly mid on, for his valuable 17. The partnership produced 148 of which Weekes had scored 135. Walsden passed the Middleton total without losing further wickets. Weekes had contributed 151, the first century by a professional in the Wood Cup Final.

I asked, "If Weekes scored 151 not out, why was Jim Wilkinson awarded Man of the Match?"

The answer came, "Weekes was expensive and his bowling was expensive as well. They scored 92 off him you know." The scorecard records that Weekes bowled 43.5 8-ball overs, 10 maidens, 92 runs and 9 wickets. He took Middleton's last 4 wickets for 7 runs. The club balance sheet shows Ronnie Wood's match fee was £10. Weekes was paid £20 for the early rounds and £40 for the Final. Any other contributions came from *Wilty* and the Chairman.

The local press carried the following:

So the game which was to have started at Rochdale on July 26, was concluded at Werneth on September 1. The Walsden players would be well advised to keep some official record of the match to show their grandchildren - verbal evidence will take some believing.

At the ceremony, surpassing any Wembley presentation for sincerity, Mr William Wood - brother of the founder of the competition, the late Ald John Henry Wood - presented skipper Len Moss with the cup.

Wilty was not invited to the celebration dinner and at the next AGM, early in 1955, The President, Chairman, Secretary and Treasurer were all replaced. There is nothing of an explanation in the club minutes. So it's not only the Yorkshire CCC committee that works in mysterious ways. It is known however, that the drawn out final took its financial toll. Ronnie Wood was released the following season and veteran Jimmy Hatchman was signed for £7 per match.

One wonders whether the card skills Weekes learnt during the long running saga were why he became bridge champion of Barbados.

I still don't understand why Jimmy was awarded *Man of the Match*. I think it should have been given to the bloke who stood on Ronnie Wood's foot.

Final gate receipts   £220.7s.6d.

From
The News and Advertiser

By engaging that faultless batsman Everton Weekes as deputy professional for the Wood Cup matches, the Walsden committee showed admirable foresight, for the "prince of cricketers" assured the club of a place in league history. It may not be generally known that Weekes' performance in the final at Werneth established three records—he was the first professional to score a century in a Wood Cup final, the first to take nine wickets in a final and his 151 was a record for the ground. In the semi-final against Milnrow, Weekes gave the amateurs a chance to shine, the performances of Sutcliffe (46) and Coupe (six for 37) contributing much to the victory.

Results   First round   Bye
            Second round   Littleborough 178 - Walsden 230
                    pro W.F. Cockburn, Australia
            Semi-final   Milnrow 111 - Walsden 151 for 6
                    pro A.E. Rhodes, Derbyshire and England
            Final   Middleton 220 - Walsden 224 for 7
                    pro Eric Price, Lancashire

Weekes' averages

Inns	N/O	High Score	Total	Average
3	1	151	280	144

Overs	Maidens	Runs	Wickets	Average
94.4	22	197	16	12.31

Walsden Wood Cup Final Team
Jimmy Wilkinson is second from the left, bottom row

6 - Not so serious

Drawing by Clive Hetherington

Huddersfield to Hollywood
Matt Ottey

Whilst links between Huddersfield and Hollywood are few and far between, both possess appealing features. Hollywood offers bright lights, fame, stardom and wealth, as well as other slightly more questionable activities, whereas the Dearne Valley countryside offers peace and tranquillity, a sense of community and of course, Nortonthorpe Cricket Club.

Yet an actress, born and raised in Clayton West, Scissett's neighbouring village, is proving that a Yorkshire girl can cut it on screen with the very best, and I do mean quite literally, the very best.

The lady in question is Jodie Whittaker, daughter of ex-Huddersfield Central League President and Nortonthorpe's hardworking groundsman Adrian Whittaker.

Jodie has been an actress for as long as she can remember, perhaps not always in front of playhouse audiences (as she did when performing in the play *Bash* at the Trafalgar Studios), or in front of millions on the TV and cinema screens (Jodie has enjoyed success in TV dramas *Doctors* and *Dalziel and Pascoe*, and the feature films *Venus*, *St Trinians* and upcoming Nazi stage show adaptation *Good* starring *Lord of the Rings'* Viggo Mortensen), but in her head she was always performing "I played on my own for hours. I didn't need anyone. All my dolls and teddy bears had a voice. My bed was a boat; my window was a magic mirror."

Jodie burst on to cinema screens with a stunning performance as Jessie in 2006's critically acclaimed drama *Venus*. Having grown up in Scissett, the role of brash young Yorkshire lass enabled her to retain the natural accent that distinguishes her so well "I'm very proud of my accent and it's a huge part of who I am. My dad would kill me if I lost it."

Although Jodie currently lives in London, her accent only gently carries a southern manner, giving way to the stronger, more familiar northern tones. Her down-to-earth character (which Adrian Whittaker will no doubt claim is down to brilliant parenting) makes the acting seem effortless and her demeanour incredibly laid back. Whilst on the subject of her northern-ness, if there is such a thing, "If I say 'Jer-deh', nobody can tell what I'm saying, she explains, so I have to go, 'Joe-dee'. It's me London voice."

She still returns home as often as her increasingly crowded schedule will permit. Her upbringing in an avidly cricket-loving atmosphere helped forge a friendship with *Venus* co-star, legendary *Lawrence of Arabia* actor and cricket fan Peter O'Toole.

The Scarborough Trophy
David Walker

What about the oft wet and uninviting Scarborough, which can be hot and balmy and attractive, up to a point? They play cricket on the beach here, in front of *Corrigan's Arcade*, under the watchful bulk of the *Grand Hotel*. There's actually two sorts of cricket, one on hard-packed sand, recently vacated by the sea, and one on the fluffy stuff, up near the promenade, invulnerable to all but the highest tide. Playing down by the sea, apart from adjusting for the wind, requires traditional skills. Dry soft sand, however, is an altogether different and awkward surface, and demands unusual and distinctive abilities, as many a promenader-turned-spectator has come to appreciate.

The ball must be a recent purchase from one of the many tat shops to be found on the front, and as such will have plenty of nap, albeit not for long. The bat can be made of any material and today, plastic is common and serviceable enough. The size is important and small is the rule, because all players must be larger than the equipment to qualify for selection. The stumps similarly, and those the length of your average Havana cigar are ideal, only one being necessary at the non-striker's end. There is no limit to the number of players and indeed sides are not compulsory. Girls are welcome, but not taken seriously. Two or three dads and older brothers are advisable to see fair play as beach cricket can be emotional and accompanied by tears and an irrational desire by the bat-and-ball owner to return home prematurely. The seniors don't field as they tend to be breathless and portly, being in receipt of long lunches. Attire varies, but footwear is often discarded. There are as many bowling styles as there are players, but the stock delivery is the full toss. If it is allowed to bounce, it simply stops and nestles inconveniently in a divot. This bowling necessitates a shorter pitch than is customary and about ten yards or less is average. Fielding is random and chaotic and unrelated to the events at the wicket. Diving, catching and running all take place with free abandon and the ball can often be ignored. Runs are taken and a batsman makes his ground by touching the single stump with the bat, accompanied by a clear shout of "stick". Twos are rare, but if the infield is cleared on a still day, ten or more runs can be scored whilst the youngest or wheeziest child is dispatched down to the sea.

If the smell of hot frying fat or the sound of slot machines and bingo callers does not offend, you can catch a game down in the South Bay most days of the week during the summer.

"Come on Sam, where've you been?" A ginger-haired seven-year old is a late arrival. Cudworth C of E Primary are playing Barnard Castle Prep in a match reduced to two unlimited-ball overs because of the impending high tide. As they wait their turn to bat and bowl, 20 children of various sizes are shouting or singing and roaming around haphazardly. Haphazard that is, except that they are nearly all on the leg side, the most prevalent shots being the pull and the hook. Apart from two girls that is, who are gossiping and combing their hair at first and second slip.

"Come on then, where do you want me?" Sam says to a middle-aged man at cover point.

"There," shouts the man and points to silly mid-on, where Sam immediately takes a graceful catch and is next in.

"I'm rubbish at batting," he says.

We've all heard this false modesty. He adopts the classic stance: upright, head still, watchful, all concentration. With sea lapping around the bowler's legs, he hits the winning run, nearly decapitating his older sister filing her nails at mid-on.

And so Cudworth took the Scarborough Challenge Trophy for the fourth time in five years.

"I like to give these North Yorkshire toffs a good stuffing," said Sam, celebrating after the game in *Corrigan's* amusement arcade.

Me and Anne!
Samantha Shilton

Every member of Upper Hopton CC will be tuning in to BBC1 this Thursday as first-team player Tom Wilks appears on popular TV show *The Weakest Link*.

Wilks, 23, is something of a local celebrity, and everybody at the club is quite excited at the thought of seeing him on TV. But Wilks is keen to play it down:

> I didn't even get the chance to talk to Anne, she wasn't bothered. She just said, 'You are the weakest link, goodbye,' that was it. I got knocked out in the second round because I was the only person to get one of my questions wrong that round, which was sort of fair enough. The question was a bit of a tricky one though, 'In food, what is the name of the celebrity chef who coined the phrase 'Doing a Delia?' I'd never have guessed that it would be Delia Smith herself who would have said it so I took a guess at Jamie Oliver. Unfortunately, nobody else got a question wrong so I was voted out.

But this is not the first time that Wilks has tasted fame. He has also previously auditioned for *The X Factor*. "That one wasn't quite as much fun, I didn't get to sing in front of the judges because you've got to sing to a room of producers first, and I didn't get past that stage. So I was out first round that time!"

Not So Serious

His time on *The Weakest Link* was short lived and enjoyable, "I originally applied for the show online, and then I had to go for an interview at a hotel in Leeds, called Bewleys. Played a little game and that in front of a camera, got through and then I got a phone call saying I was going to be on in February."

"It was being filmed at Pinewood Studios in London. They put us up in a really nice hotel and, yeah, it was a good experience, really good experience. And I did right well in the first round, got two questions and banked some money right before the buzzer so I'm pretty proud of that."

Robert Holdsworth of the first team insists that the club support him 100%. "We'll all be watching on Thursday of course. There might have been a few jokes made but it's all lighthearted and we're chuffed for him."

It's a great day for being a boy
David Walker

One September Sunday in 2004, Almondbury Casuals CC, a very friendly cricket club, visited Upperthong. The match was not about a result or performances, though there were some. All that really mattered were the upper reaches of the Holme Valley, bathed in warm Indian Summer sunshine, and playing cricket. It has to be said that balmy weather and Upperthong do not often go together, exposed as it is to vicious storms that sweep down from Holme Moss.

Two youngsters played for Upperthong that day, one on the pitch with his dad and the other in the car park. It got me thinking of all the young lads over the years who have knocked about at cricket. Strange games reminiscent of those informal pastimes played before rules were invented and written down.

Such impromptu occasions are part of the preparation for formal cricket. They are also important lessons in the art of growing up. Take the average domestic backyard or school playground. It is here where juniors sharpen their competitive edge against marauding older brothers and pale fifth formers with nicotine-stained fingers.

At school, a minimal set of kit is essential and old and knackered is preferable. Don't take that dark brown heirloom, signed by Len Hutton, discovered after days of rummaging in the attic, or you will never see it again. Balls must be bald. Stumps are dangerous and on no account must they be used; wall and chalk is quite sufficient. The track will vary from rough and stony to hard uneven clay and there must be no fear of body contact as several hundred matches are played simultaneously, side by side. Bad light and rain-stopped-play are rare. Indeed a wet ball can be an advantage as it leaves a distinctly visible trace on chalk and clean bowled cannot be disputed.

Drawing by Clive Hetherington

Lbws are, however, extremely contentious in this style of cricket, as they can be in the more orthodox forms. It's a battleground, where a talent for survival is swiftly rewarded. Being able to play with a plank for a bat and a ball that barely bounces is clearly valuable, but think of the benefits accruing from attempting to retrieve a square cut from an irate *5-Remove* psychopath whose knuckles scrape along the floor.

In the back garden, the object of the game is not to lose the ball. It's all about defence and occupying the crease, much to the frustration of older brothers. They in turn respond by changing the rules to suit them.

"Owzat?"

"Not out, you dollop."

"How come, it 'it off stump."

"It never, look here there's a mark on't door frame."

"We said t'door frame were going to be off stump."

"Did we 'eck."

Another nine year old stamps his feet and walks back to his mark next to the clothes post. Apart from batting for days, his main weapon is the donkey drop, lobbed as high as his bedroom window, pitching as a half-volley some thirty seconds later, just outside the line of off

Not So Serious

Me an' our kid

stump. But he must choose his time carefully. He must wait for the moment when older brother's eyes wander and glaze, that instant when concentration has moved internally to Maxine Hargreaves, her with the big charlies down at number seven. What did he see in her?

Got 'im. The ball sails away to long-off, into Mr Grumps' potato patch, where it will stay until autumn, that bit of the year when the harvest gives birth to hundreds of chewed moth eaten tennis balls.

"Six an' out, you're out." The nine year old does an impression of an aeroplane in an acrobatics display. Older brother stands bemused, wondering whether he's been had. This is chess, where tactics and planning, capitalising on strengths, minimising weaknesses, patience, a strong nerve and sheer native wit are cultivated. And, when there are no more balls, David and Goliath will go and find another game to play.

That September Sunday in 2004, two boys played for Upperthong. One played on the pitch with his dad; a bowler of promise, a first-ball duck and a steep learning curve. The other, fully present and correct in whites, helmet, pads and gloves played in the car park between two sets of full-sized metal stumps that came up to his shoulder. A left-hander, he played alone during the Casuals' innings, straight driving, blocking, square cutting and taking quick singles. Every so often he would pause, and turn and look at the action out in the middle. After a minute or so he would turn away and get back down to the business at hand.

And the match result?

Upperthong more than 250 for 6 off 35 overs

Casuals   190 all out in 34 overs

Upperthong Cricket Ground
Daniel Stewart

The rural setting of Upperthong Cricket Club is excellent; a vast expanse of countryside with few trees. Apart from the walls around the site, there are no obscuring features. The pitch seems to blend in perfectly with the views beyond, the green of the turf and the hills forming on the other side of the Holme Valley.

The journey to Upperthong Cricket Club feels perilous due to the twists and turns in the road leading up to the ground. It helps create the air of rural isolation: few homes this far up; no houses overlooking the ground, as at many clubs; and wonderful views of the Holme Valley.

(Upperthong was founded in 1999 and play in the Huddersfield Central League)

Stewart Larner, An Almondbury Casual
David Walker

In 2003, Greg Smith was Chairman of the Almondbury Casuals Cricket Club, a very friendly cricket club. One Sunday he described to me the purpose of the club as "specifically to give hopeless cricketers a game." I'm unsure what Stewart felt about his talent, but the neutral observer would have to say he was not a gifted cricketer. I first met him when he worked as an NHS clinical psychologist in Manchester. Clearly no slouch in the brain department then. There are many who are not entirely sure what a clinical psychologist does and despite working with

Not So Serious

several, I confess I haven't much of a clue either.

Stewart was a jolly chap, a *Billy Bunter* character. Rumour had it the Casuals got him on a free transfer from Cambridge Methodists, a friendly team just off the Bradford-Leeds bypass, near the Leeds-Liverpool Canal. Whatever the pace or age of the bowler, he wore a helmet. He went to Yorkshire's winter nets every year where presumably he learned, as a prelude to each Casuals innings, to run four laps round the square before returning to the changing room to practise his shots, a sort of air guitar with a cricket bat. A routine he never varied.

I first saw him play in the 2004 Yapham fixture. Stewart batted six  and came in to join opener Paul *Nozzer* Brown, who, despite a number of runs going begging wide of his leg stump, being dropped four times and overthrown on at least one attempted run out, was still at the crease and well on his way to a hundred. Stewart somehow stayed with Nozzer and helped him to finish on 96 not out. In the last over, Nozzer was so desperate to get the ton, he lapped Stewart once, could have been twice, trying to run a four. Stewart couldn't speak for ten minutes.

At the winter committee meeting of 2005, Will Ward, opening bat and surveyor, told this wonderful story about Stewart's indoor net. Stewart lived in a large old vicarage, with attics and cellars. Somewhere in the depths was an open space 22 yards long with a wicket at one end. A Heath-Robinson construction began at the other. Made of rifled guttering of a diameter suitable for a cricket or tennis ball, it angled downwards for fifteen yards before letting go with speed and accuracy. A seemingly innocent descent thus transformed an angelic orb into a satanic missile. As fiendish a delivery that ever spat off a length. And Stuart would be there, waiting …

The following spring, fresh from winter coaching, I watched him against Whitley Bridge. His helmeted innings started with the conventional forward press, but pretty soon we saw boundaries from the slog-sweep, pioneered by Lance Kleusener but now taken to a new height.

Higher still, the lob wedge to short midwicket and finally the classic thick top edge to backward of square. 11 runs and pleased as *Punch*. But it didn't stop there. Following the tea interval, Stewart showed us the discipline it takes to play at his level. Four times round the square and several stretches had jaws dropping in the pavilion, making way for the last pieces of chocolate cake. Then his over of slow off-spin was pure mystery. His fielding came from the much vaunted ataxic school of coordination. No one was in the slightest doubt as to the outcome when a short skier entered his area of the pitch. But then he caught it.

Stuart's retired from the NHS to Scarborough, and he is in the process of forming his very own team.

Cricket Rules
Lee Hughes (Ms)

Played on a pitch complete with two wickets
twenty-two men play traditional cricket
The first team that's in for the start of their innings
bat from the centre from the beginning
Trying to get a boundary ball shout
the other team try to get them all out
All batsmen don pads to every shin
and when everyone's out the others are in
Umpires sport long coats and white hats
batsman's on crease complete with his bat
Bowler's balls are made of fine leather
spinning them fast or slow or whatever
Fielders catch balls along the deep edge
at silly mid-on or out at long leg
By striking the ball the batsman can run
but if he's caught out he'll no longer be on
Each of the teams have an innings apiece
winner's the one with most runs when games cease

7 - Postscript

Drawing by Clive Hetherington

Not the end, it just felt like it
(My son the cricketer part III)
David Walker

I needed some consolation.

My son, Chris, had represented the town; a week-long festival when the sun shone every day. We won three and lost one. He was Man of the Tournament at the local six-a-sides. Belted Holmfirth off the park in the league. Last match of the season, not out and going well. Needed four to be the league's highest scoring batsman. The coach shouted down from the pavilion balcony, "Stay in Chris, don't get out." What happened next? It'll be on *Question of Sport*.

The coach, not Flyn, chose him as Player of the Year. He didn't turn up to collect the award and hasn't played since. A slow bowler of promise and an attacking left hand bat. Fifteen years old with a lifetime of cricket ahead him. It's a bit like an arthritic joint. I can still feel the pain on a bad day.

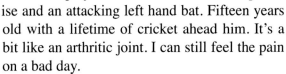

When Chris first picked up a bat, I built a cricket net up on our top field. A worn out gazebo frame draped with used tennis and football nets, stitched together into a cricket tunnel. The track was more or less twenty-two yards, uphill with a slight dip in the bowler's run up. It was pretty flat apart from a sporting exposed fir tree root on a full length. Our house was at long on, the neighbour's garden was in the covers and the farmer's fields were at midwicket and long stop. I always knew when it was time for a net by the sound of the motor mower starting up.

It was not fun back-garden cricket. We had full protection and it was competitive. I had to dig in and remember my long lost forward press. The shoulders lose it with age, so my bowling was a struggle and Chris got plenty of opportunities to play shots. It was a father and son rite of passage thing, but it also kept me in some sort of batting nick.

It was a lonely day when I packed away the netting and took it to the tip. I wasn't going to grow old watching Chris score hundreds for Yorkshire.

Then there was Mr Moult. He played for Elvaston, a beautiful Derbyshire cricket club, and I played against them, for Almondbury Casuals. We fielded first and Mr Moult came in at five down, a first-teamer returning from injury. Medium height, heavily built, a young muscular Colin Milburn. He repeatedly belted the ball in my direction with no intention of running. If and when I got a hand to the ball all I could do was deflect it. For twenty embarrassing minutes I was reduced to retrieving the ball from the boundary. Later, when I went in at seven, Mr Moult was brought on to bowl. Just for a fitness test they said. When not on his days off, he opened the first team bowling. He started his run up just in front of the sightscreen and thankfully kept it pitched up. The sound of breaking wickets was not long delayed, followed by a sad and long car drive home.

It's time to go when the number of embarrassments and mistakes exceed the number of successes. When the guffaws of team-mates begin to matter. My second retirement from cricket.

The first time I was about the same age as Chris. Selected for a team of fifth form tearaways two years older than me. I kept missing straight ones and they were never going to coach and support someone who was keeping out one of their pals. As Dad watched my exam results rather than my forward press, he was happy for me to walk away.

Triple grief. Two teenagers who would never play cricket to their full potential, and a hopeless old romantic. It wasn't the end of anything, it just felt like it.

Flyn would have shook his head and smiled.

Final Innings

Lee Hughes (Ms)

Remembering ball on willow
my innings now is done
I've 'played the game' in every way
and boy I've had some fun

I've bowled some maidens over
in the art of the noble game
Had some ups and weathered downs,
and claimed my bit of fame

I've played the field and been caught out
but stole the finest catch
A man no longer standing
now I've played my final match

But as the umpire calls me
it's to God's own pitch I run
Picked for the heaven eleven
now my earthly life is done

Authors

Ashley Ball is a former Sports Journalism & Media student, University of Huddersfield.

Craig Bamford is a former Sports Journalism & Media student, University of Huddersfield.

David Brenchley is a former Sports Journalism & Media student, University of Huddersfield.

Mike Butler is the author of 'From Batley to Barnsley: A History of the Heavy Woollen Cricket Challenge Cup 1883-2005' (2006).

Dan Barton is a former History student, University of Huddersfield.

Martin Bishop is the author of 'Bats, Balls and Biscuits: A Brief History of Cricket at the Reading Biscuit Factory' (2008).

Matt Carswell is a former Sports Journalism & Media student, University of Huddersfield.

Sam Christie is a former Sports Journalism & Media student, University of Huddersfield.

Jane Crane is a local cricket enthusiast.

Richard Crouch is a former History student, University of Huddersfield.

Zak Data is a former Sports Journalism & Media student at the University of Huddersfield.

Mark Edmonds is a former Sports Journalism & Media student, University of Huddersfield.

Russell Eggar is a former Sports Journalism & Media student, University of Huddersfield.

Matt Elston is a former Sports Journalism & Media student, University of Huddersfield.

David Febrero is a former Sports Journalism & Media student, University of Huddersfield.

Aaron Gales is a former Sports Journalism & Media student, University of Huddersfield.

David Galley is a local cricket enthusiast.

John Garnham is a former Sports Journalism & Media student, University of Huddersfield.

Stuart Greenwood is a lifelong supporter and official of the former club Mytholmroyd Methodists CC.

Andrew Hardcastle is a cricket and rugby league historian. He is the author of 'Lost: The Former Cricket Clubs and Cricket Grounds of Halifax and Calderdale' (2005).

Rob Hardie is a former Sports Journalism & Media student, University of Huddersfield.

Brian Heywood is a co-author, with Freda and Malcolm Heywood, of 'Cloth Caps and Cricket Crazy' Upper Calder Valley Publications (2004).

Ian Hirst is a former Sports Journalism & Media student, University of Huddersfield.

Ian Hodgson is a former Sports Journalism & Media student, University of Huddersfield.

Sam Hollis is a former Sports Journalism & Media student at the University of Huddersfield.

Martin Howe is a cricket enthusiast and writer.

Lee Hughes is a former Creative Writing student, University of Huddersfield, and author of 'Wielding the Willow: An Anthology of Cricket Poems' (2007).

Tony Hutton is a cricket enthusiast based in Leeds.

Chris Knowles is a former Sports Journalism & Media student, University of Huddersfield.

Dominic Kurreen is a former Sports Journalism & Media student, University of Huddersfield.

Jean Margetts is a local cricket supporter.

Rob Light wrote his PhD doctorate on cricket in the nineteenth-century West Riding. He worked on the Calderdale and Kirklees Cricket Heritage Project in 2004 and 2005.

Tony Lister is the author of 'You Couldn't Make It Up! The Complete History of Burnley Cricket Club 1834-2008' (2009).

Toby Lock is a former Sports Journalism & Media student, University of Huddersfield.

William Marshall is a Phd student, University of Huddersfield.

Pat Neal is the Secretary of Mirfield CC and author of 'George Herbert Hirst: Mirfield Cricket Club 1891' (2006).

James Norbury is a former Sports Journalism & Media student, University of Huddersfield and co-author, with Pat Neal, of 'Thanks to the

Inghams: Stories of Mirfield CC' (2008).

Dennis O'Keefe is a Phd student of cricket history, University of Huddersfield and author of 'Start of Play' (2007).

Jon O'Shea is a former Sports Journalism & Media student, University of Huddersfield.

Matt Ottey is a former Sports Journalism & Media student, University of Huddersfield.

Roy Pearce is the author of 'Gentlemen and Players: Wirksworth Cricketers 1757-1914' (2007).

Andrew Pearson is secretary of Thurstonland CC and the author of the club's history.

Paul Rai is a former Sports Journalism & Media student, University of Huddersfield.

Muni Rashid is a former History student, University of Huddersfield.

Peter Redding is a former Sports Journalism & Media student, University of Huddersfield.

Duncan Robinson is a former Sports Journalism & Media student, University of Huddersfield.

Colin Shakespeare is a cricketing poet.

Samantha Shilton is a former Sports Journalism & Media student, University of Huddersfield.

Matthew Skirving is a former Sports Journalism & Media student, University of Huddersfield.

Andrew Smith is President of Illingworth St Mary's CC and the author of the club's history.

Daniel Stewart is a former History student, University of Huddersfield.

Allan Stuttard is an ex-player, raconteur and committee man at Walsden CC.

Gareth Thompson is a former History student, University of Huddersfield.

Michael Ward is a former Sports Journalism & Media student, University of Huddersfield.

Mark Whitcombe is a former History student, University of Huddersfield.

Dave Wooding is a former Sports Journalism & Media student, University of Huddersfield.

Media

Elspeth Milnes qualified (honours) in fine art following retirement as a theatre nurse at Scarborough Hospital. She is now a freelance artist.

Clive Hetherington gained an honours degree in 1968 and worked as a physicist and computer scientist. Since retirement he has taken up drawing, painting and ceramics. He also sings in a male voice choir.

Richard Turner LRPS is an enthusiastic local photographer who relishes indulging his passion on his favourite game. A some time player and many time watcher.

Sue Brant is a cricket artist.